Hazrat Nizamuddin Auliya

RAZIUDDIN AQUIL is Professor, Department of History, University of Delhi. His research and teaching interests encompass religious traditions, literary practices and political cultures in medieval and early modern India. He is the author of several books on Sufism and many other aspects of Indian history, including *Days in the Life of a Sufi: 101 Enchanting Stories of Wisdom* (Pan Macmillan, 2020).

Hazrat Nizamuddin Auliya

BELOVED OF GOD

RAZIUDDIN AQUIL

PAN

First published 2026 by Pan
an imprint of Pan Macmillan Publishing India Private Limited
707 Kailash Building, 26 K. G. Marg, New Delhi 110001
www.panmacmillan.co.in

Pan Macmillan, The Smithson, 6 Briset Street, Farringdon,
London EC1M 5NR
Associated companies throughout the world
www.panmacmillan.com

ISBN 978-93-6113-243-8

1 3 5 7 9 8 6 4 2

Typeset in Guardi LT Std by R. Ajith Kumar, New Delhi
Printed and bound in India by Thomson Press India Private Limited

FSC
www.fsc.org
MIX
Paper | Supporting responsible forestry
FSC® C010615

Musalman wa hindu wa tarsa wa gabr
ze khake darat jumla afsar kunand
Chu kafur-o sandal az aan khake paak
be-chashm andar aarand wa daair kunand

Muslim, Hindu, Christian and Magi
make a crown out of the dust of his threshold
They apply the sacred dust like camphor and sandal
in their eyes and circumambulate the shrine.

– Amir Khwurd Kirmani on Hazrat Nizamuddin's *dargah*, as quoted in *Siyar-ul-Auliya*, fourteenth century

For

Sufi souls devoted to love for God

and service to humanity

CONTENTS

PREFACE

Hazrat Khwaja Nizamuddin Auliya (1238–1325) is one of the finest Sufi figures to have flourished in India since the thirteenth century. Hazrat Nizamuddin's tomb, located in Delhi in a neighbourhood named after the saint himself, is an important pilgrimage site for people of all faiths, a veritable centre of the sacred geography of Sufi spirituality or Sufism in India. The saint belonged to the first cycle of the five great Sufi masters of the popular Chishti spiritual lineage or *silsila* (order), which flourished in India in the thirteenth and fourteenth centuries. Before him, the Chishtis were led by towering religious personalities like Khwaja Gharib Nawaz Muinuddin Chishti of Ajmer, Khwaja Qutbuddin Bakhtiyar Kaki – after whom the Qutub Minar in Delhi is named – and Khwaja Fariduddin Ganj-i-Shakar, undivided Punjab's foremost Sufi saint. Hazrat Nizamuddin's successor in the Chishti order, Shaikh Nasiruddin Chiragh-i-Dehli (1274–1356), became immortal in the city's popular memory for keeping the *chiragh* (lamp) burning at night at a time when the despotic Sultan Muhammad Tughlaq (ruled 1325–51) was forcefully changing the capital of the Sultanate from Delhi to Daulatabad (Deogiri in the Deccan), leaving Delhi desolate.

Hazrat Nizamuddin was born and brought up in the bustling city of Badaun (now in western Uttar Pradesh) in a Syed family (descendants of Prophet Muhammad) that had immigrated from Bukhara in Central Asia. He was brought up by his pietistic mother, Bibi Zulaikha, having lost his father early. Nizamuddin moved to Delhi to pursue his higher education, specializing in the traditions of the Prophet, Islamic jurisprudence and Perso-Arabic literature and history. After his studies, he spent some time looking for a government job as a *qazi* (judge) before being introduced to Chishti Sufism. He soon became an outstanding disciple of Shaikh Fariduddin Ganj-i-Shakar. In decades to come, Hazrat Nizamuddin grew into a living legend, eventually becoming something of a patron saint of Delhi.

Hazrat Nizamuddin's teachings and detailed accounts of his life are available in the authorized collection of his *malfuzat* (spiritual conversations), titled *Fawa'id-ul-Fu'ad* (Morals for the Heart). This collection, compiled by a close disciple and mystically inclined poet, Amir Hasan Sijzi (1254–1337), over a period of fifteen years, had become a popular text in his own time. The period covered in the compilation coincided with the reign of Sultan Alauddin Khalji (ruled 1296–1316), whom Hazrat Nizamuddin famously did not consent to meet despite the sultan's many demands. Significantly, both Amir Hasan Sijzi and the saint's closest disciple, Amir Khusrau (1253–1325), were in the service of the sultan, but Nizamuddin wished for critical distance between the political and spiritual domains. He had famously remarked, 'I have two doors in my house, if the sultan forcibly entered from one, I will vacate it from the other.'

Hazrat Nizamuddin had a difficult time with two other Delhi sultans as well – Qutbuddin Mubarak Shah Khalji (ruled 1316–20) and Ghiyasuddin Tughlaq (ruled 1320–25). But both rulers died untimely and violent deaths at the time they were harassing Hazrat Nizamuddin. Later, Chishti's memory celebrates their elimination as an obvious result of the saint's curse. At the same time, the

Chishti Sufi tradition also celebrates the bestowal of kingship by Sufi masters to the more competent and deserving persons.

Through his teachings, as recorded in *Fawa'id-ul-Fu'ad* and in later *tazkiras* (hagiographies), especially the well-known collection of biographies, *Siyar-ul-Auliya* (Lives of the Friends of Gods) by another disciple, Amir Khwurd Kirmani, Hazrat Nizamuddin educated his followers in the Sufi way of loving God. This was expressed through service to humanity, which was considered to be the highest form of prayer. In doing so, the saint, like his Chishti predecessors, was presenting a tolerant and peaceful face of Islam, which sought to bring non-Muslims into its fold without using force or invoking political power. Thus, even if Sufis like him were not against the conversion of non-Muslims, they believed reform within required more urgent attention. In their understanding, the dichotomy in the moral integrity of people professing Islam – that is, not sincerely following the precepts of Islam to become good human beings – was a more serious matter than winning over new converts. Eventually, a huge non-Muslim population did embrace the Islam of the Sufis in many regions with substantial concentrations of Muslims, as in Punjab, Bengal and the Deccan.

By presenting a face of Islam that was tolerant, accommodating and peaceful, singing songs of love and making charitable endeavours, the Sufis were able to excel in an environment marked by spiritual competitiveness with holy men of different hues. They attracted large numbers of followers of all religions all over the Indian subcontinent. And even today, visitors to the shrines of these Sufis are never checked for their caste, creed or gender. Large numbers of visitors to the Nizamuddin shrine, respectfully referred to as *dargah* or *darbar*, are non-Muslim, and a significant number are women. The keepers of the shrine pray in Urdu: *sabke jayez armaan puray hon* (may lord fulfil everyone's legitimate aspirations).

The spiritual environment of Hazrat Nizamuddin's tomb complex is considered a liberating experience. Some visitors do not even seek blessings and *mannat* (benediction) but visit because deep veneration for the saint's grace and charisma holds an important place in their hearts. This veneration is powerfully voiced by the accomplished *qawwals*, whose ancestors have sung songs, highlighting and celebrating the greatness of the khwaja for over seven centuries now. He is addressed from early in his career as Sultan-ul-Mashaikh (Sultan among the Sufis) and

Mahbub-i-Ilahi (Beloved of God). Though his given name was Muhammad bin Ahmad (Ahmad being the name of his father), the name Nizamuddin itself was miraculously attached to him, as was the title, Auliya (plural of *wali*, a friend of God). Nizamul Auliya wad-Din is shortened to Nizamuddin Auliya, which means administrator of friends (of God) and faith of Islam.

This book is a product of my long-standing interest in Sufi literature of the Delhi Sultanate, especially the *malfuzat* of Hazrat Nizamuddin Auliya. I gratefully remember the kind support and encouragement of several eminent professors, which has kept my interest in the subject going. I especially remember Syed Jamaluddin, Syed Muhammad Azizuddin Hussain Hamadani, Narayani Gupta, Muzaffar Alam, Dilbagh Singh, Harbans Mukhia, Satish Saberwal, Partha Chatterjee, David Curley and Werner Menski.

A large number of colleagues and friends have also provided moral support for my lasting dedication to the subject. Grateful thanks are due to Arupjyoti Saikia, Tilottama Mukherjee, Rashmi Mishra, Manish Kumar, Deeksha Bhardwaj, Bharati

Jagannathan, Geeta Arya, Sanal Mohan, Amit Dey, Parul Pandya Dhar, Fatemeh Samavati, Kumari Khushboo, Farhat Nasreen, Jaya Kakkar, Mohammad Ali, M. Nisar, Rafiullah Azmi and Gulfishan Khan.

In what follows, in this book, details from the life and teachings of Hazrat Nizamuddin Auliya will be presented for the appreciation of scholars and devotees needing to know more about the saint. In his lifetime, Hazrat Nizamuddin was known to be aware of what was inside the heart of his disciples even when it was not expressed verbally. In my case here, as a historian of Sufi traditions, my interest is in bringing together some fascinating aspects of the extraordinary life of the much-venerated saint in his own spiritual and political context. I am grateful to the team at Pan Macmillan – especially Rajdeep Mukherjee, Prasun Chatterjee, Pujitha Krishnan and Shreya Ahlawat – for their keen interest in publishing this book, which sums up the accounts of excellence in the conduct of the fine soul – Sultan-ul-Mashaikh Mahbub-i-Ilahi Hazrat Khwaja Nizamuddin Auliya of Delhi.

Raziuddin Aquil
University of Delhi

1

INTRODUCTION: BELOVED OF GOD

Aye aatish-i firaaqat dilha kabab kardeh
Sailaab-i ishtiyaaqat jaanha kharab kardeh

The fire of separation has roasted the hearts, making them kabab
The overwhelming desire has destroyed many lives, making them kharab.

– Hazrat Nizamuddin Auliya, quoted in *Fawa'id-ul-Fu'ad*

The vast corpus of Sufi literature in a variety of languages, forms and genres help us understand the critical social, cultural and political roles Sufis have performed through the ages. The literature especially draws attention to ethical concerns Sufis insisted on to make themselves and their followers acceptable in the eyes of their merciful and loving God. Sufis considered themselves friends and lovers of God and strove to cultivate awe-inspiring credentials. The main tenets of Sufism were love for the eternal divine and respect for all His creations, whether humans or non-humans and irrespective of caste, creed or gender. Compassion and some humanism were encouraged. The focus here is on the spiritually imbued conversations of the foremost Chishti Sufi saint of Delhi, Hazrat Khwaja Nizamuddin Auliya, in *Fawa'id-ul-Fu'ad*, a famous text compiled by Amir Hasan Sijzi.[1]

The reading of the text (*Fawa'd-ul-Fu'ad Khwani*) is a regular feature at the *dargah* of Hazrat Nizamuddin, during his annual *Urs* or death anniversary. Literally translating to wedding or marriage, *Urs* of Sufi saints is celebrated with the assumption that they spent their lives devoted to God and went after death to be near him. Indeed, Nizamuddin had willed that his funeral procession should accompany *qawwals* singing songs of love as in a *sama* (musical assembly of Sufis). This would have been a major deviation from tradition, creating difficulties for the *ulama*, the dominant Sunni–Hanafi theologians and custodians of customary practices in Islam. Therefore, some prominent disciples decided not to follow the will of the departed Sufi shaikh, and Nizamuddin's own funeral procession did not include music.

The study of medieval and early modern Indian history has flourished with continued scholarly investments over the last century. Some of the best scholars of medieval Indian history are also the finest historians of Sufism in medieval India. These include Mohammad Habib, S. Nurul Hasan, Khaliq Ahmad Nizami, Saiyid Athar Abbas Rizvi, Carl W. Ernst and Bruce B. Lawrence. They have highlighted the significance of the kinder face of Islam practised by Sufis, which played an important role in emphasizing the value of pluralism and diversity in society.[2] Another set of historians such as Simon Digby, Richard M. Eaton and Muzaffar Alam have expanded the field further with their rigorous scholarly and professional approach to the study of the past.[3] Recent decades have witnessed the publication of new research, revealing further layers of intricacies in the history of Sufism. This is particularly so for the research and publication of Nile Green, Scott Kugle and Mikko Autere, among others.[4]

Other notable scholars of the history of the Sultanate period in the last hundred years or so include I. H. Qureshi and Aziz Ahmad, both writing from a clearly identifiable perspective of Muslim separatism in the middle of the twentieth century.[5] As history writing gets trapped in the political turmoil, right-wing political propaganda takes it to its nadir, with an otherwise professional historian, K. S. Lal, going on to claim that medieval India under Muslim rulers was a dark age, because there was no electricity in medieval India. For Lal, this was so because medieval Islamic governing principles and actions were based on the Qur'an, which was against science, leading to its suppression. He would conclude that much of the evils facing Indian society today are the legacy of Muslim rule in India.[6] Such wild assertions are made with more aggressive determination in what are now known as the dubious 'WhatsApp university' forwards. Away from the bizarre attack on academic history, historians have continued to work with scholarly rigour to produce more credible histories. These include, for the Delhi Sultanate, important works such as those published by Peter Jackson, Sunil Kumar and Blain Auer.[7] The lists of distinguished scholars of the histories of the Deccani Sultanates and Mughal India are equally long and formidable.[8]

The accessibility and use of wide-ranging source material has meant newer explorations in areas – questions, regions and periods – which were hitherto neglected. Primary sources for the history of the Sultanate period are available in abundance. Newer sources are continuously being discovered and deployed. Historians are also going back to conventional sources such as court chronicles and literary compositions in Persian. These include significant early writings of medieval stalwarts like Minhaj-us-Siraj Juzjani (1193–1260), Ziyauddin Barani (1285–1357) and Amir Khusrau.[9] Literature in a number of Indian languages is also being used by historians now with some degree of confidence in their use as reliable sources for the writing of history. Traditionally used coins and inscriptions remain important, the latter are specially studied with the built heritage for much sophistication in understanding the context and meanings in their forms, shapes and influences. With several layers of entangled pasts, sites like the Qutub complex, Feroz Shah Kotla and Purana Qila in Delhi are threatened by recent political contestations. This issue requires care and responsibility on the part of the political domain. This is especially so as public culture is becoming increasingly volatile.

A large corpus of Sufi literature is still attracting historians who can read Persian as well as medieval vernaculars. Persian texts in a variety of genres include theoretical treatises, *malfuzats*, *maktubats* (letters), *tazkiras* and mystical poetry (especially poetry of love, or *ghazal*).[10] Well known, but not properly studied or utilized by scholars of Sufism, are the *premakhyana*, or the poetry of love in Hindi.[11]

It is important to have a quick look at some of the main features of Sufism in the medieval period before getting into the details of the anecdotes (*hikayat*) on ethical and moral conduct in Sufism, as narrated by Hazrat Khwaja Nizamuddin Auliya in *Fawa'id-ul-Fu'ad*. Nizamuddin belonged to a chain of the powerful and charismatic spiritual leadership of the Chishti Sufis of the Delhi Sultanate. His predecessors included Khwaja Muinuddin Chishti of Ajmer, Khwaja Qutbuddin Bakhtiyar Kaki of Mehrauli in Delhi and Khwaja Fariduddin Ganj-i-Shakar of Punjab. Khwaja Nasiruddin Chiragh of Delhi, Nizamuddin's successor, completed the chain of the first five great Chishtis of the Sultanate period.[12]

Love for God and service to humanity are central to all forms of Sufi traditions, practices, *tariqats* (orders) and their *silsilas* (branches). This requires complete cleansing of the lower self (*tazkiya-i-nafs*) and cultivation of the heart (*qalb*). Unconditional and excessive devotion in love for God (called *ishq-i-haqiqi* or *ishq-i-ilahi*) is compared with Majnun's madness for Laila. Yet Sufis thought that they were more intelligent than Majnun, who wasted his life over Laila, who died, whereas the God they loved was eternal. Further, since God is supposed to have created everything, love and respect for all his creations are equally important. Service to humanity (*khidmat-i-khalq*) is then extended to plants and animals as well. The most touching reference is of God forgiving the foremost early Sufi figure, Rabiya of Basra in Iraq, for she used to feed a stray dog outside her house every night. Provocatively, she would also go around the town during the day, carrying a bucket full of fire in one hand and a bucket full of water in the other. Rabiya would complain that people were engaged in prayers for fear of hell and the reward of heaven. She wanted to destroy both hell and heaven, so that people would pray for the love of God and not for those promised rewards or punishment.[13]

Sufi spiritual exercises brought the practitioners close to God to the extent that there were moments when they thought there were no differences between the human soul of the Sufis and the merciful and loving God. These were expressed through concepts such as unity of existence and unity of witness (*wahdat-ul-wujud* and later *wahdat-ul-shuhud*), which meant there is no difference between God and human beings, and alternatively, one can merge into the Great God. The public elaboration of such experiences of nearness to God, to the extent of imagining getting merged into him, was discouraged. Mansur al-Hallaj, a Persian mystic and poet, is the best-known example of this. An ecstatic al-Hallaj had claimed that he represented the truth of God or probably God himself, *Anal Haq*. His utterances were bordering on heresy in Islam, and he was executed by the orders of the caliph in Baghdad.

Nearness to God also meant Sufis could acquire supernatural abilities to perform miracles (*karamat*), which were to be hidden and sometimes used for the benefit of people, which has historically made Sufi institutions, especially their *dargahs*, popular. Indeed, miracles as a source of benevolence have garnered interest in Sufi traditions across regions and time periods. Sufi traditions recognized other kinds of miracles as well. These included the extraordinary marvels of the prophets (*mu'ajizat*), which needed to be spectacularly performed, paranormal abilities of non-Muslim mystics such as the *yogis* (*istidraj*) and low-quality tricks (*ma'unat*) of magicians and other evil doers.

Sufism was influenced by various sources and often appropriated practices and traditions from outside Islam. While this did draw people from other religions to Sufism, it also meant Sufis were suspected of crossing the rigid boundaries marked by the theological custodians of Islam. On their part, the Sufis were clear about the path they were following and for its purpose. In their attempt to know God and achieve nearness to him, they were seen to be following the path shown by the Prophet of Islam and the early exemplars. Thus, remaining within the fold of Islam in the probable chain of *shari'at* (customary law in Islam), *tariqat* (mystic path), *ma'rifat* (spiritual knowledge) and *haqiqat* (the truth of the loving God), with the *shari'at* being the bottom line on which failure to follow the mystic path was judged.

Hazrat Nizamuddin Auliya feared what hell a Sufi would fall into if they were not bound to the laws of Islam, whatever the jurisprudence or sects (*mazahib* or *maslaks*). This meant that the obligatory rituals of *namaz*, *roza*, *zakat*, *hajj*, etc., were necessary ingredients or spices of the Islamic meat curry. The meat, or the most important ingredient in this curry, was the Sufi style of distancing themselves from the world (*tark-i-duniya*). Prayers were of various types, including night-long recitation of the Qur'an, chanting recognized formulae to remember God (*zikr*) and listening to fine poetry in musical assemblies (*mahfil-i-sama*), with *qawwali* growing into a fine Sufi music genre.

Unlike 'heterodox' mystic groups in Sufism, such as Qalandars and Madaris, the Chishti Sufis conformed to the traditional Islamic norms of conduct.[14] Their non-conformism was limited to their defiance of the rigid interpretation of Islam by the *ulama.* Besides other aspects of their religious or spiritual practices, which were often questioned by the *ulama, sama* and *qawwali* were a cause of major tension between the Chishti Sufis and the *ulama* in the Delhi Sultanate. For the Chishtis, music was central to their expression of love for God, but the Hanafi *ulama* condemned song and dance techniques in Sufi spirituality as forbidden or *haram.* Sources talk about various forms of music recommended in the Sufi circles of the Delhi Sultanate as well as their arguments defending its legitimacy. Sufis referred to classical sources of Islam (such as Qur'an and traditions associated with Prophet Muhammad) that defended the use of music amidst the *ulama's* clamour for its suppression. Hazrat Nizamuddin Auliya's practice of organizing *mahfils*, the Sunni Hanafi theologians' opposition to music and the resultant inquest at Sultan Ghiyasuddin Tughluq's court had taken an ugly turn, but Nizamuddin defended his interest in music with a lot of grace.[15] This defence is discussed in detail in Chapter 9.

Sufis were also open to the adoption of non-Muslim spiritual practices, with texts such as the *Amritkund* and *Rushdnama* showing common grounds shared in Sufism and other spiritual traditions. Practices such as breath control (*pranayama*) and meditations influenced by *yogis* and *sadhus* (such as *chilla-i-ma'kus*, the practice of hanging upside down for forty days as practised by Baba Farid) would attract negative attention from the *ulama*, but Sufis had no issues sharing practices with *yogis* and Sants. These appropriations have a longer history, going back to Central Asia and Khurasan, where forms of Buddhist practices were also in vogue. Later, spiritual figures such as Kabir and Eknath were asking: did God make a mistake in making someone a dog or *kafir*, for that matter?[16] All these would mean that the visitors to *dargahs* transcended distinctions of caste, class, creed and gender, as well as respect for the difference between human and non-human beings.

Sufis created conditions for peaceful community relations in diverse neighbourhoods, which were ensured by responsible politics and broad-based governing principles. Charitable endeavours by Sufis included running *langar*s or community kitchens for feeding the poor as well as healing rituals, for the physical and mental health of people in places where medical facilities were abysmal or non-existent. The Sufi concept of renunciation meant living among the people and serving them, while staying away from worldly greed. Sufis were expected to eat minimally, particularly avoiding non-vegetarian food, for several reasons, including respecting sentiments of large numbers of Hindu devotees (probably preventing any suspicion of mixing beef). This is because beef-eating had emerged as a contested issue in medieval India. For some, not eating meat also took care of sexual desires that were assumed to be caused by red meat. It also helped maintain long hours of ritual purity through ablutions (*wuzu*).

Accounts of avoiding eating (fasting) as part of spiritual exercises or wholesome feeding of visitors to Sufi hospices (feasting) abound in medieval Sufi texts. Thus, there is a striking contrast in the merits of eating less or fasting for forty days of meditation (*chilla*), and the virtues of offering rich platters of food to guests. These included *tahiri*, *qorma* and *firni*. And, if nothing was immediately available, at least a glass of water was to be served on arrival. Feeding visitors was explained in simple terms: guests not offered anything to eat will feel like they have visited a graveyard where the persons buried cannot offer anything to eat.

2

KINDER FACE OF ISLAM

Ba 'ashiqan nashin o gham-i 'ashiqi guzin
Ba har ke nist 'ashiq kam shau ba u qarin

Embrace love's longing in the company of lovers
Avoid those who do not understand the
language of love.

– Hazrat Nizamuddin Auliya, quoted in
Fawa'id-ul-Fu'ad

Sufism presents a kinder face of Islam. Its central tenets focus on love for God and service to humanity – ideas and practices followed by Prophet Muhammad. These facets of Islam are often overlooked or ignored, especially in today's times when certain narratives about Islam overshadow the rest. There is a lot of ignorance about all these, which need to be corrected with some emphasis, especially in our post-truth era. It is important that well-researched works by serious historians and other responsible scholars are brought to the fore rather than letting propaganda shape history. Invoking Sufism in this context will help.

It is not difficult to explain the essence of Sufism. It is about love for God and respect for all His creations, rising above all the distinctions of castes, creeds, gender, etc. In this worldview, even animals and plants are to be respected as marvellous creations of God. Sufism calls for complete and ecstatic devotion to God, yet service to humanity is considered the best form of worship in most Sufi traditions. Worldliness and materialism are disapproved, and withdrawal from lust and desire is recommended. Since Sufism is about love and devotion, it is also about matters of the heart, which need to be cultivated for a person to become an evolved human being. This is achieved through prayers, vigils, fasting and chanting recommended formulae. Such a heart also longs for poetry and music to remember God. Music and dance thus become an important part of Sufi practice, making it a vibrant spiritual movement across geography and history.

Though the Sufis would often face opposition from the *ulama*, and their political masters – the rulers, medieval sultans – all three parties respected each other's presence, power and authority. Sufism and the Bhakti movement both recommended ambiguity in matters where clear boundaries could not be drawn and believed that strict opposition would result in violent conflicts. An invocation to peaceful coexistence was considered the favourable way forward.

Sufism has historically spread to all parts of the known world. Wherever the Sufis went, they embedded themselves in local customs and practices. They played important social and cultural roles in shaping and transforming society with their message of universal brotherhood, egalitarianism, tolerance and respect for difference. The focus of the research of this writer has been on the significant presence of charismatic Sufi masters of mainly the Chishti tradition through the medieval and early modern eras. Later custodians of this tradition have continued to show that the *mazars* and *dargahs* of Sufis remain relevant in modern times. A large majority of Muslims in India follow peace-loving Sufi-oriented Islam, and at the same time, a large majority of visitors to Sufi shrines are non-Muslims!

It is about transcending politically controlled religious boundary markers, which Sufis also defied.

There are many Sufi orders, spiritual lineages or *silsila*s, of which Chishtis, Qadiris, Suhrawardis and Naqshbandis, and their sub-branches such as Firdausis, Shattaris and Mujaddidis are especially well known in India and abroad. These primarily came to the subcontinent from the Middle East, Iraq, Iran and Central Asia through the medieval period. In the last couple of centuries, Indian Sufism has travelled worldwide to spread in parts of Africa, Europe and North America. Various strands of Indian or south Asian Islam – with all their diversities and intellectual and cultural excellence – have represented Islam worldwide as flag-bearers and examples of what it means to be Muslim. At the same time, Sufi traditions acquired deeper roots in large parts of the subcontinent.

There are many records and several studies relating to Sufism in central and southern India. In fact, in current research, some of the finest works on Sufism in India are about the Sufi traditions and practices in the Deccan region since the fourteenth century, at least. Scholars such as Richard Eaton, Carl Ernst, Nile Green and Scott Kugle have published significant new research on various important dimensions, both mystical and social, related to the vibrant Sufi traditions located at historic centres such as Aurangabad, Khuldabad, Bijapur and Gulbarga. Burhanpur was also a major Sufi centre since the arrival of Islam and Sufis in those parts in the thirteenth century. Similarly, Kerala and Tamil Nadu have a long tradition of Sufi-centric popular religiosities, associated especially with invocations to Abdul Qadir Jilani Ghaus-i Azam Pak, who is considered the father of all Sufis. The origins of Sufism in South India can be traced back to its contact with the medieval Arab world, though some strands of north Indian Sufism also travelled southwards through the medieval period. Along with these, Punjab in the west and Bengal in the east complete the sacred geography of Sufism in the subcontinent. Islam in what is now Bangladesh is simply unimaginable without its introduction to Sufism through charismatic figures such as Shah Jalal Mujarrad of Sylhet and a host of other Sufi masters settling down around the thirteenth century, if not earlier.

As mentioned earlier, Sufism advocates for peaceful coexistence. This is especially important in our troubled times when narrowly defined religious boundaries and aggressive religious politics are creating a serious humanitarian crisis. Politicians and extremist groups who thrive on violence are creating fault lines between communities and pitting them against one another in the name of religion and community. The Sufi message of peace among all offers an alternative for hope. *Sajjadanashins* (spiritual successors of Sufi saints) and spiritual leaders of Sufi shrines are keeping the traditions of Sufi teachings alive. They have kept the gates of shrines open to visitors and followers, including women, non-Muslims and the poor, besides thugs, criminals and ministers, who also seek blessings and benediction, offering flowers and ritual Sufic *chaadars*, especially on the *Urs* of saints.

Sufism has managed to remain a popular spiritual movement across centuries, despite all the cultural shifts it brought with it. It has defied fundamentalist pressures from within Islam while also attracting people from other religions who might simply be curious about Sufism. The Sufi recommendation for continuous soul-searching, cleansing one's heart of all evil and proper conduct even in the most atrocious situations, are virtues for a life lived with grace. A'ishah al-Ba'uniyyah, of fifteenth-century Damascus, emphasized in her treatise on the principles of Sufism on *taubah* (repentance), *ikhlas* (sincerity), *zikr* (remembrance) and *muhabbat* (love). *Zikr* and love for God are also powerfully reiterated in Sufi *qawwali*.

Qawwalis attributed to Amir Khusrau, who was a close disciple of Hazrat Nizamuddin Auliya and a much-respected father figure in classical Hindustani musical tradition, still touch the heart of people with a *zauq*, or taste for spiritual pleasure. *Qawwali* performances by such modern stalwarts as Nusrat Fateh Ali Khan, Abida Parveen, Zila Khan and Sanam Marvi, among many other practitioners, entertain devoted connoisseurs and cater to popular tastes. Notice several of them are women practitioners who command a lot of respect, and some of the best ones are located in what is Pakistan today. Though a large number of people throng to *dargahs* for blessings, it is the powerful and melodious renditions of the *qawwals* which have kept the belief in Sufi traditions alive. They have continued to sing songs of love even in times and places full of hate. The custodians of Islam, the *ulama*, have long doubted the legitimacy of Sufi musical assemblies, *mahfils*, including the participation of women and the use of instruments. Sufis have defended it as part of their *zikr*, or remembrance of God.

Some anecdotes from Sufi literature will

illustrate its focus on humanism further. Sufi literature includes *malfuzat*, *tazkiras*, mystical poetry and treatises in several languages. Here, we refer primarily to *Fawa'id-ul-Fu'ad*, a compilation by Amir Hasan Sijzi of conversations at Hazrat Nizamuddin's hospice (called *jama'at-khana*, which was a smaller establishment, compared to the *khanaqah*, or monastery-like complex owned by the more resourceful Sufis). Amir Hasan was a friend and colleague of Amir Khusrau in the service of the Delhi Sultanate. Ziyauddin Barani has written in his *Tarikh-i-Firuz Shahi* that Amir Hasan was known in his own lifetime as the Sa'di of Hindustan (equivalent to the Persian poet Sa'di of Shiraz in Iran). Some anecdotes recorded by him in *Fawa'id-ul-Fu'ad* are presented below.

On the Excellence of Knowledge and Steering Clear of Political Regimes

Once, a young scholar visiting Hazrat Nizamuddin told him that he had completed his education and had started hanging around the sultan's court, seeking employment to support himself. When he was leaving, the khwaja recited this couplet:

She'r dar wasf-i haal bas sirrahe ist
Chun bekhwahish rasid maskhare ist

Poetry can be a fine expression of ecstatic emotions
But it becomes a joke if used for fulfilment of greed.[1]

Nizamuddin remarked that poetry is a fine art, but if it is used to sing praises of people without distinction, it loses its excellent flavour. Similarly, knowledge is a great thing in itself, but if it becomes the source of livelihood for which a scholar has to beg from door to door, it loses the respect it should command. Political patronage, positions and jobs are to be especially avoided, for they will always demean and exploit and even kill.

Most Sufis wanted to steer clear of the political regime, maintaining critical distance, and yet in some contexts guided political regimes as well. Not for nothing that people in government send *chaadars* to *dargahs* during the annual *Urs*.

On Respect for Women and Daughters

Amir Hasan has recorded that his long-term servant, a former slave named Malih, had brought some sugar candy (*nabaat*) for Hazrat Nizamuddin, as one of his four daughters was married off (*'aqdi shudeh bood*). When the khwaja was offered sugar candy, he inquired what the occasion was (*algharaz chun nabaat bedid, farmud ke chist*).

Amir Hasan submitted that Malih's daughter had gotten married. The khwaja turned to him (Malih) and said the birth of a daughter creates a *hijab* or veil between the father and hell. Malih was four times protected from hell as he had as many as four daughters (*har ke ra yak dukhtar baashad u ra hijabi baashad az dozakh, tura khud chahaar ast*)!

The khwaja then remarked: *abul-banaat marzuq; pedare dukhtaraan ra wus'ati baashad dar rizq* (fathers of daughters are provided with an increased sustenance and livelihood). In other words, God provides daily bread and subsistence for girls; they are not supposed to be a burden on anyone, they do not need to be killed and should be respected for what they are. This kind attitude of Sufis is different from the general patriarchal treatment of women in Muslim societies at the time. Sufis spoke in gender-neutral terms and maintained ambiguity on homoerotic attractions. They may not have been feminists and considered Sufi practices as acts of *mardanagi*, or masculine prowess.

In conclusion, hundreds of such anecdotes continually reaffirm Sufi emphasis on humanism, mercy and tolerance of difference. Reiterating this, the khwaja recited this couplet:

> *Har ke ma ra yaar nabud izad u ra yaar baad*
> *Wa aanke ma ra ranjeh daarad raahatash bisyaar baad*
>
> Someone who can't be friends with me, let God be his friend
> And the one who annoys me, should be at great ease and comfort.
>
> *Har ke u khaari nehad dar raahe ma az dushmani*
> *Har guli kaz baaghe umarash beshagufad bi khaar baad*
>
> If anyone put thorns on my path out of animosity
> Every flower in the garden of his life remains thornless.[2]

Hazrat Nizamuddin explained that if someone puts thorns in your path and you do the same in retaliation, there will be thorns everywhere. He added that generally people are good with the good and bad with bad, but Sufis are good with good people and good with bad ones also (*miyane mardumaan hamchunain ast ke ba-naghzaan naghzi o ba-*

kuzaan kuzi, amma miyane darweshan hamchunain ast ke ba-naghzaan naghzi o ba kuzaan ham naghzi).

As a patron saint of Hindustan, Khwaja Gharib Nawaz Muinuddin Chishti preached that the best form of prayers included: listening to the grievances of suffering people, helping the needy and feeding the hungry. The khwaja had also said that people with the following three characteristics could legitimately be considered as friends of God: river-like generosity, affection like that of the sun and modesty and hospitality of the earth. None of them discriminate in what they have to offer. It's not for nothing that people from all walks of life, rising above narrow religious and political boundaries, have continued to flock to his *dargah* for 800 years now.

Similarly, the *dargah* of Hazrat Nizamuddin Auliya was thronged by people of all faiths within twenty-five years of his passing. A mid-fourteenth century biography of Hazrat Nizamuddin, *Siyar-ul-Auliya* by Amir Khwurd Kirmani, has quoted a verse anticipating the latter-day pluralistic slogan of unity and brotherhood of communities of people across religious divides:

> Muslim, Hindu, Christian and Magi, all of them,
> make a crown out of the dust of his threshold;

They apply the sacred dust like camphor and sandal
in their eyes and circumambulate the shrine.[3]

3

ETHICAL EXCELLENCE AMIDST THE UGLINESS OF THE WORLD

Gar nik aayam mara az Ishan girand
Dar bad basham mara badishan bakhshand

If I am noble, I may be counted with them;
If I am bad, I may be forgiven on their behalf.

– Hazrat Nizamuddin Auliya, quoted in *Fawa'id-ul-Fu'ad*

Constant vigil on moral conduct and seeking forgiveness from God are critical features of Sufism. The focus of this chapter will be the conversations of the foremost Hazrat Nizamuddin Auliya, in *Fawa'id-ul-Fu'ad,* on this topic. The anecdotes or *hikayats* presented in some detail address a spiritual fraternity of people with a heart (*ahl-i-dil*), which was soaked in love for God and everything around. As Nizamuddin Auliya said, dervishes (members of Sufi orders) were seen to be so graceful in arguing their case that people wondered how elegant they might be when expressing their love for each other. Examples of conversations between Nizamuddin and his followers, given below, will further establish the emphasis on moral and ethical conduct in Sufism as well as the complete submission to the will of God.

Nizamuddin Auliya once told his audience that Prophet Muhammad had foretold that the five generations (*tabaqat*) of people after him, with each of the generations lasting for forty years, would gradually fall into ruin. The first generation was that of the companions of the Prophet (*sahaba*). They were a fine set of people known for their spiritual knowledge and contemplation (*'ilm* and *mushahida*). The second generation comprised the companions of the companions of the Prophet (*tabi'in*), who were noted for their good deeds and piety (*birr* and *taqwa*). The third generation consisted of people who let the good things of the world go to people who desired to have them, and they shared everything for the love of God. Such characteristics were marked by attempts to make contact and connections with people with a sense of compassion (*tawasul* and *tarahum*). As the situation would deteriorate further from the point of view of Islamic piety, the fourth generation would include people who would resort to aggressive animosity (*khusumat*) to misappropriate everything, identified by cut-throat competitiveness (*taqato,* literally to cut). Analogous to it would be the conduct of the people who surreptitiously hoarded wealth, not sharing with others and turning their backs on others (*tadabur*, from *tadbir* or strategy for mindless self-interest at the cost of everything else). The fifth generation would constitute people who thrived in anarchy and chaos (*harj-o-marj*). They would kill each other to feed their self-interests, brutalizing and killing each other in manners identified with wild beasts (*gusht-o-pust-i yakdigar uftand o dar kushtan-i yakdigar shawand*).

Thus, such would be the characteristics of the people two centuries after the time of Prophet Muhammad. Nizamuddin observed that after those 200 years, the situation would have deteriorated so much that the birth of a pup would be better than the birth of a human being (*agar kasi sagi bachche bizayad beh, na farzand-i-adam*). The Sufi master concluded that two centuries after the Prophet were long gone, so they could imagine the situation today, that is, the early decades of the fourteenth century. With tears in his eyes, he concluded, what could one say about the characteristics of our time (*in sa'at-i khwud mardum che guyad*).[1] In contexts like the above, Sufis could take a high moral ground through their superior conduct and nearness to God.

Sufis also thought they could perform better miracles than other non-mystics, such as *yogis*, who were treated as inferior. Some Sufis maintained a clear distance from the *yogis*, yet others engaged with them in discussions and even performed miracles together. A few anecdotes involving such interactions will illustrate the nature of dialogues and competitiveness in the spiritual domain.

Sufis believed some mystics could fly in the air, and they displayed this paranormal ability when provoked to do so. Nizamuddin Auliya narrated an account of such a challenge faced by Shaikh Safiuddin Gazeruni from a Yogi at Uchchh, in Sindh. The Yogi confronted Shaikh Safiuddin and suggested a contest of levitation between them, that is, they would perform the miracle of flying in the air (*baya qadam be-namayam*). The shaikh told the Yogi that since he was the one making such claims, he should perform the feat (*shaikh guft da'wi tu mi-kuni tu qadam be-nama*).

The Yogi elevated himself off the ground and remained suspended so high in the air that his head touched the roof. Thereafter, he descended straight to the floor and challenged the shaikh to repeat the miracle. Shaikh Safiuddin raised his head towards the sky and prayed to God: you have blessed others with this skill, bestow to me also the ability to perform this miracle. Soon the shaikh was seen flying in all four directions – from west, to north and then to south before returning to the place where he sat. The Yogi was bewildered. He prostrated before the shaikh and confessed that his power was limited to performing straight elevation in the air and that it was beyond his capacity to take right or left turns. Marvelling at the shaikh's ability to fly in various directions, the Yogi admitted that the shaikh's practices were true and divinely ordained and his own practices were false.[2] Sufi literature abounds in such narratives of encounters with *yogis* in which the latter are shown to be defeated and the superiority of Sufis is displayed.

Another account involving Sufi–Yogi conversations takes an interesting turn when Bibi Fatima Sam of Delhi suggested that Nizamuddin could marry the daughter of someone known to her. Fatima Sam was a formidable Sufi figure, personally known to Nizamuddin's preceptor, Shaikh Fariduddin Ganj-i-Shakar, and commanded a lot of respect. Saying no to her would be an embarrassment to both her and Nizamuddin. So, the latter told her of his meeting with a Yogi who was visiting Shaikh Fariduddin's hospice at Ajodhan, Pakpattan, now in Pakistan. The Yogi had made a proposition that the character of a child was determined on the day the child was conceived. Different days of the month had different characters assigned, and twenty-nine to thirty different kinds of characters were already determined. The Yogi suggested that some people did not know the right time to have sex, and that is why sometimes useless creatures were born (*farzandan keh bi-zauq bairun mi-aayand az an ast keh marduman waqt-i mubasharat na mi-daanand*). On hearing this, the veteran Fariduddin scolded young Nizamuddin for wasting his time in such matters. Sufis were wary of yogic tricks, and Nizamuddin was meant to grow in the mystic path and therefore was wedded completely to God. Fatima Sam understood the message that Nizamuddin could not concern himself with matters of love and marriage, and withdrew the proposal. Marriage is a recommended practice in Islam, but many Sufis thought they could not handle the responsibilities that came with it and therefore remained unmarried (*mujarrad*).[3] Their nights were spent in prayer, meditation and in remembering God, and their days were spent in service to followers, devotees and various visitors to the hospice, such as the *yogis* as we saw above.

Once, there was a discussion at Nizamuddin Auliya's hospice about people kissing the hands of dervishes in anticipation of receiving blessings (*khalq dast-i darweshan mi-bosand o barkat mi-talaband*). Nizamuddin offered the perspective from the other side: dervishes who offer their hands for kissing wish and pray that they get the hands of a blessed person to hold![4] Sufis had also realized that since so many people kissed their hands and prostrated before them, it was also possible that some antagonists would throw stones at them. This could perhaps be as part of a divine strategy to keep them grounded and in balance (*mizan*). Sufis would take such attacks gracefully, with *jamal*. But if the nature of opposition was perceived as devious, demonic or satanic, they needed to be suppressed with a heavy and wrathful hand, with *jalal*. Sufis could, it was believed, break the neck of the detractors and even curse them to be dispatched to hell! Hence, most people had wished to be on the right side of the Sufis, seeking blessings and benediction, and soaking themselves in the language of love and belonging of the spiritual kind.

For people visiting Sufis seeking amulets (*ta'wiz*) to combat different kinds of mental or physical illness, Shaikh Fariduddin's advice to Nizamuddin was to not turn anyone away. The simple formulae for the amulets to cure illnesses were to inscribe *Allah-o Shaafi, Allah-o Kaafi, Allah-o Ma'afi*. If amulets and relics worked, Sufis would get the credit; if not, God was supposed to have planned otherwise. Complete and graceful submission to the will of God was the recommended ideal.[5]

In the most aesthetically sophisticated forms developed through centuries of practice, Sufism teaches the virtues of tolerance and peace. For, after all, the Sufis sought to preach what they practised – love for God and respect and service to humanity. Enduring pain, cultivating grace and guarding himself against any evil, Hazrat Nizamuddin prayed to be counted amongst the best of the people, saintly exemplars of the larger Muslim world.

4

FASTING AND FEASTING

Spending one dirham on getting food prepared and sharing it with friends for eating together is better than giving away 20 dirhams in alms to the needy.

– Hazrat Nizamuddin Auliya quoting a saintly person, *Fawa'id-ul-Fu'ad*, p. 63

Recalling the days of penury in early life, Hazrat Nizamuddin once told his disciples that on nights when his family had nothing to eat, his mother pretended to cook something on the stove, assuring her children that they were guests of God that night. The children liked the idea and looked forward to being served by God, even though they would sleep hungry, waiting for food to arrive. Later in life, Nizamuddin lamented that the innocent childhood pleasure of the idea of being guests of God provided a different degree of satisfaction altogether. Sufis celebrated *faqiri* (poverty) in the mystic path, with complete submission to the will of God (*tawakkul* and *qin'at*). They believed they were following the path of Prophet Muhammad, who is known to have proclaimed: '*Al-faqro Fakhri.*' Poverty is my pride.[1]

The rule for visitors at Nizamuddin's *jama'at-khana* was: *salam* (greetings), *ta'am* (eating) and then *kalam* (speaking). Immediately offering something to eat was prioritized, even a glass of water, or else it would feel like the guest was visiting a graveyard where the buried cannot offer anything to eat. These rules came from accounts of the life of the Prophet. His companions visiting him would be served bread and dates, among other things, as a matter of regular practice. They were not allowed to leave without having some of these (*nani ya khurmai ya chizi digar ta na-khurdandi baaz na-gashtandi*).[2]

Sufis recommended chanting the name of God (*zikr*), listening to fine poetry (*qawwali* and *sama*), and conversations with friends on the mystic path – eating and listening to music together. There were norms for proper conduct for all these. Possible violations were discouraged, and if occurred, needed correction.

Shaikh Shahi Muye Taab, a saintly figure of the thirteenth-century Badaun (now in Uttar Pradesh), once went out with friends for a picnic. His friends prepared food, including *khir*, a heady concoction of milk, rice and sugar flavoured with some dry fruits and herbs. When food was served, Shaikh Shahi pointed out that there had been a misappropriation (*khiyanat*) in what was being served. Perhaps two of the fellow companions had secretly consumed some of the milk, which was considered a serious misdemeanour. When questioned, the two accused submitted that the milk had overflowed while boiling, and they consumed only that much. They asked, what were they expected to do, let the overflowing milk go to waste? Shaikh Shahi replied that their consuming milk secretly and lying about what happened was wrong, irrespective of the circumstances and rejected their explanation. By way of punishment, the two of them withdrew from the group and stood in the sun till they started sweating profusely. Shahi then called for a barber and declared that he would like to bleed as much as his friends had sweated. The condemned friends had to endure the punishment for their greed, and, in return, the Sufi wanted to suffer because they were friends, after all. Thus, justice was done with the commitment of friendship intact![3]

In Sufi fraternities, friends were also advised to avoid catching the evil eye when gathered or travelling together. And, when they fought, they did it with much civility and grace (*jamal*). People wondered if they quarrelled so politely, how gorgeous they might be while loving each other.[4] In contrast, dealing with antagonists was a tough business. They were to be wrathfully shut up (*jalal*) with violent performance of miracle (*karamat*), the power for which was derived on account of the Sufis' nearness to God.* In an episode, a contemporary Sultan, Qutbuddin Mubarak Shah Khalji, is reported to have ordered his nobles not to visit Nizamuddin and not donate any money in unasked-for charity (*futuh*) there. This was to stifle funds for running the public kitchen, *langar*, at the latter's hospice. In response, Nizamuddin ordered his servant and caretaker of his hospice to increase both quantity and items in the

* Nizamuddin Auliya identified the powers to perform miracles as *mu'ajizat* (prophetic marvels), *karamat* (Sufi miracles), *istidraj* (yogi's paranormal performances) and *ma'unat* (evil tricks by magicians), according to *Fawa'id-ul-Fu'ad*. Sufis gave some credit to Yogis for their mystical abilities but were wary of them as they were not Muslims.

menu: *tahiri, qorma* and *firni*. It was believed that the money for the expenses was miraculously arranged. The conflict was over the sultan trying to force Nizamuddin to participate in dinner parties held at his court, which the latter avoided. The matter was settled with the brutal murder of the sultan by one of his own close associates. Nizamuddin's followers believed that his curse had led to the elimination of the sultan. The Sufi's charismatic mother was also involved in the encounter. He had gone to visit her tomb and prayed for his protection from the aggressive sultan.[5] In general, the relations between the Sufis and rulers tended to remain ambiguous and varied depending on the traditions and practices of particular Sufi orders (*silsila*s).[6]

Sufis were needed by their disciples and the general public for their charitable endeavours, including *langars*, feeding the poor and helping them with money. The saliva-infused food leftovers of Sufi saints were taken as sacralized material (*tabarrukat*) by their disciples, part of the belief in Sufi healing practices. Often, someone asking for help was given less, and the ones not opening their mouth for help were generously supported. All of these were considered as pain, which needed to be endured: serve people to please God. This was interpreted as renunciation (*tark-i-duniya*). This required austerity and moderation in eating. Formal prayers, though accepted as obligatory, were not enough beyond a point. For Nizamuddin, *tark-i-duniya* was not about renouncing all material wealth, becoming naked and living in a cave. It was wearing clothes (*libas bepushad*) and eating food (*ta'am bekhurad*) but steering clear of greed and hoarding.[7] Referring to the taste of renunciation, using the metaphor of taste (*lizzat*) of food, and recommending higher moral ideals of freedom from greed, Nizamuddin suggested honourably rising above worldly desires (*himmat buland bayad kard*). This meant refusing bad food as well as bad conduct (*sar khisi*) in anticipation of receiving better things (*chizi sharifi*).[8] It is recorded that once food was being served in Nizamuddin's *majlis* (spiritual assembly), one person present there remarked that he had visited a place where *tutmaaj* (thin slices of pasta, vermicelli) was served and even though he was full, he ate that to his satisfaction. The man said similar things in appreciation of good food. Nizamuddin replied that he once went to the house of Shaikh Jamaluddin Hanswi (of Hansi, now in Haryana). It was a winter morning, and Jamaluddin turned to Nizamuddin and recited this couplet:

Ba-roghan-i gao andarin ruz-i khunak
Niko baashad harise wa naan-i tunak

With cow ghee on this cold day,
Pottage and *paratha* will be so good.[9]

Sufis recognized the value of good food but advised avoiding falling for greed. Nizamuddin recounted that an accomplished pietistic figure used to say that prayers (*namaz*), fasting (*ruza*), chanting beads (*tasbih*), etc., were like spices (*hawa'ij*), but the most important thing in the cauldron was meat (*gusht*), without which spices were useless. When asked to explain this metaphor further, he said, meat is like *tark-i-duniya*, which was spiced up by prayers. He added that complete distancing from the world was the ideal, with or without prayers. Nizamuddin interpreted it as, if only oil, pepper, garlic and onion were put together and boiled in water, the *shorba* (soup or curry) was fake or false (*zur* or *durugh*). Real *shorba* (*asl*) was made of meat, with or without spices.[10]

The above discussion may be summed up with a Persian couplet recited by Nizamuddin, about Sufi ideals of cleansing the lower self to rise above sensual desires and cultivating the heart for higher good, that is, love:

Yek lahze ze shahwati keh dari barkhez
Ta benashinand hazar shahid peshat

Rise above your desires for a moment
So that a thousand lovers could sit before you.[11]

Excellence of a perfect man in Sufi traditions (*insan-i-kamil*) requires self-cleansing, which includes eating less (*qillat-i-ta'am*), speaking less (*qillat-i-kalam*), sleeping less (*qillat-i-manam*) and limited interactions with people (*qillat-i-suhbat ma al-anam*).[12] Controlling eating was not difficult, as sustained phases of fasting were considered ideal and an important feature of Sufi practices. Nizamuddin once remarked that adhering to the demands of repentance was a challenge. For example, when a person decided to stop drinking wine (*az sharab tauba kunad*), his friends and companions might have criticized him (*mazahamat numayand*) and tried to take him back to the place they had the pleasure of drinking (*zauq girafte bashand*). If the person was truly committed to his repentance as a matter of cleansing his heart, he would abandon his companions rather than returning to drinking, which was a sinful act, *haram*.[13]

For such pious people, fasting was an exercise in self-control and a recommended practice. However, it was also recommended not to make it a habit. However, those who fast regularly get used to remaining hungry, and soon the pain of fasting becomes tolerable for them. According to the Sufis, the more meritorious way of fasting is one which is demanding for the self and the body (*nafs*). One such practice of fasting is called *ruza-i-da'udi*, in which the practitioner intermittently fasts for a day and eats the next day. This could prevent fasting from becoming an easy practice. This was also in line with an observation related to the Prophet: someone who fasts all the time has neither fasted nor eaten (*min sam al-dahr la-sam wa la-aftaar*). Thus, there were conditions attached to it.[14] Normally, fasting during the month of Ramazan and for two days of every month (thirteenth and fourteenth of the lunar calendar, called *ayyam-i-biz*) would suffice. This is what Nizamuddin Auliya recommended to Amir Hasan Sijzi, the compiler of his *malfuzat*.[15]

At the same time, strict fasting, contentment and the power of patience were considered virtuous, for all these were part of spiritual distancing (*tark*) and experiments (*tajrid*). Nizamuddin narrated the account of a dedicated dervish who practised such mastery of hunger that his stomach pressed against his back. On days he had eaten something (such as *kanjareh*), he would not accept any money or food. In doing so, he surprised people with his extreme integrity (*sidq*), contentment (*qin'at*) and power of patience (*quwwat-i-sabr*).[16] Another account referred to a trader who fasted for twenty-five years (possibly abstaining from eating anything from dawn to dusk) without anyone knowing it. People at home thought he had eaten something in the shop, and while in the shop, they thought he must have taken a meal at home. In such cases, according to Sufi wisdom, people look at the practice (*'amal*) and intent (*niyat*). If their intent was aimed at receiving God's grace, even small prayers were liked by Him. Excessive deference to piety and prayers was not required.[17]

Referring to the merits and demerits of eating even when full, Nizamuddin suggested that eating even when one's stomach was full was valid in two situations: first, when someone who is hosting a guest eats even when full, hoping that giving company to the guest will encourage the latter to eat, is valid (*jayez*); second, when those fasting know that they have no provision for an early morning meal (*sahri*) can eat even when full so that they will not remain hungry for a longer period than the stipulated hours from dawn to dusk.[18]

On the other hand, Sufi traditions marvelled at the fortitude of the practitioners such as Bibi Aliya, a saint in Delhi in the fourteenth century. She practiced *chilla*, locked in a room with just a few cloves to sustain herself and she would not eat of them either. Aliya was the spiritual preceptor of Delhi's despotic sultan, Muhammad Tughluq.[19] As a prince, Tughluq was also a devotee of Nizamuddin Auliya. This was the time when his father, Sultan Ghiyasuddin Tughluq, was harassing Nizamuddin, until the former died suddenly in a tent which came crashing down, not far from Delhi. Sufi fraternities believe this was due to Nizamuddin's curse. The sultan had ordered Nizamuddin to vacate Delhi, and the latter had famously retorted: *hunuz dilli dur ast* (Delhi is yet far away).*

* This remark of Nizamuddin was first recorded in an early-fifteenth-century text, *Tarikh-i-Mubarakshahi* of Yahya Sirhindi. *Diilli dur ast* later became a popular proverb for taking up a challenge, especially when dealing with Delhi's tough politics.

Muhammad Tughluq created difficulties for Nizamuddin's close disciples who did not follow all his dictates. The sultan wanted to force Nasiruddin Chiragh-i-Dehli, Nizamuddin's successor in the Chishti order of Sufism, to eat in his *darbar*. Eating in his court would be a grave error, according to the Sufis. Piety without regard for a *halal* source of income was a waste and could be considered a deception caused by some satanic forces. But keeping in mind the sultan's violent temperament, Chiragh-i-Dehli obliged him, taking a small quantity of *shorba* from a spoon in his hand.[20] Thus, an exception was made as the sultan's income, based on loot and violence, was not considered to be *halal*, or legally permissible.

Nizamuddin once related a story of a young man who became a disciple of Ibrahim Adham, an early Sufi saint of Balkh (in Afghanistan), and impressed the latter with his piety and devotion. The saint was surprised that even though he lacked the commitment to prayers, he was able to discover from the light of his enlightened self-consciousness (*be-nur-i zamir-i raushan*) that the *shaitan* (devil) was working behind him. The man ate from an unlawful source of income and the *shaitan* kept him busy in prayers to cover up the sin he was committing. Knowing this, Ibrahim Adham asked the man to eat what Adham ate. The man began to eat food cooked in dervish style, in this case, from money collected by selling wood. Soon, the deep devotion he was involved in was gone to the extent that even the obligatory prayers became demanding for him, which he merely did for show. He was, however, able to hold on to the struggle and eventually succeeded in surviving on the path of righteousness (*kaar-i aan jawan saakhte shud o be-sidq baaz aamad*).[21]

Indeed, Muslim lives have historically struggled on *halal–haram* dichotomy. For reasons cultural and political as well as theological, certain commodities and ways of consuming them have been considered as *halal*, while others are abhorred as *haram* (not permissible). Beef, when processed with the recommended method, is *halal*, and so is coffee, despite its potency to think and dissent. Pork is *haram* under all conditions, and for some reasons, such as troublesome deviance, drinking wine is treated as a major sin, *gunah-i-kabira*. The defiance relating to wine drinking, poetic or real, is often celebrated in Sufi poetry, making custodians of Islam aghast.[22] As spiritual exemplars (*buzurgans*), Sufis were expected to maintain a life based on Islamic injunctions for piety (*taqwa*). Silent prayers at night and sustained periods of fasting during the days were the usual practice.

5

MERITS OF FEEDING THE POOR

Afshu as-salama wa aat'emu al-ta'ama

Spread peace and feed people.

– Tradition of Prophet Muhammad,
Sahi Bukhari

Just as fasting or minimal eating is highly recommended, generously offering food to all of God's beloved creatures, including guests, those unable to provide for themselves and even stray dogs, is much celebrated in Sufi fraternities. Many traditional boundaries are thus broken, notions of purity are defied and social hierarchies are transcended. Human–animal relations are redefined.

Sufi–Bhakti traditions have long emphasized sharing food as part of social equality, doing away with notions of taboo attached to used food, food shared within or outside castes and concern for animals.[1] Anecdotes such as Rabiya Basri feeding a stray she-dog outside her house every night and God forgiving all her sins were recommended as something to be followed diligently.[2] Respect for dogs in Islam goes back earlier, to the powerful words of wisdom of Ali ibn abi Talib, the Prophet's cousin and son-in-law. He is quoted as saying, happy is the one who leads the life of a dog! For the dog has ten characteristics which everyone should possess. First, the dog has no status among creatures; second, the dog is a pauper having no worldly goods; third, the entire earth is his resting place; fourth, the dog goes hungry most of the time; fifth, the dog will not leave his master's door even after receiving a hundred lashes; sixth, he protects his master and his friend, and when someone approaches he will attack the foe and let the friend pass; seventh, he guards his master by night, never sleeping; eighth, he performs most of his duties silently; ninth, he is content with whatever his master gives him and, tenth, when he dies, he leaves no inheritance.[3]

The quest for moral reckoning made Sufis do some fascinating experiments. Fifteenth-century Sufi,

Shaikh Ahmad Abdul Haq of Rudauli (in Awadh, in present-day Uttar Pradesh) threw a birthday party to celebrate his pet dog birthing pups. The day after the party, an eminent Sufi, Shaikh Jamal Gujari, complained about not being invited. Abdul Haq responded that only the dogs of the city were called for the feast held by his dog (*mezbani sag bud sagan ra talabidim*). He also added that according to the tradition of the Prophet, the world was like a carcass and its seekers were dogs.[4]

Starting as a Sufi and becoming one of the best exponents of medieval *nirguna* (that is, belief in a formless God) Bhakti tradition, Kabir Saheb or Sant Kabir (died 1518) is known for his strong opinions on kindness towards dogs and other species. He opposed the slaughter of chickens, goats and cows. Beef-eating had also become a controversial issue during Kabir's time. In his public proclamations, Kabir reiterated his condemnation of the slaughter of animals, especially targeting Muslim's preference for meat-eating:

> *Bakri, murgi kinh phurmaya, kinke kahe tum chhuri chalaya*
>
> Whose royal order was it to bring the goat and the hen under the knife? [5]

The saint also questioned Muslims' sincerity in their prayers and practices, linking it with a lack of kindness for animals: *din ko roja rahat hai, raat hanat hai gaai* (keeps fast during the day and gorges on beef at night).

Further, Sultan Zainul Abidin of the fifteenth-century Kashmir, who is celebrated in posterity as a majorly venerated saint, Budshah, had banned the slaughter of cows during his long rule. This political move was of interest to Mughal Emperor Akbar (ruled 1556–1605) and his court-chronicler, Ab'ul Fazl, in the latter half of the sixteenth century.[6] Vegetarianism became an aggressive ideology in centuries to come, eventually to a point where killing a human being for killing an animal was a justifiable act.[7]

Sufis were quick to adopt vegetarian food, both in private and in public, for example, in the food served in *langar*. Nizamuddin had narrated an interesting story of a renowned Sufi saint and commentator of the Qur'an, who sold only vegetarian dishes. Shaikh Usman Harwani lived in Ghaznin (now in Afghanistan), cooked dishes of vegetables such as turnip (*shalgham*) and beetroot (*chuqandar*) and sold them. However, buyers would often give counterfeit coins (*darm-i-qalb*) for what they bought. Shaikh

'Usman knew the coins were fake, but did not say anything, letting customers go. This went on for so long that the community thought that the Sufi had no idea of the distinction between fake and real coins (*qalb-o-sara*). As the time of his death approached, Shaikh 'Usman raised his head towards the sky and prayed to God. As he was most knowing, people gave him fake coins and he accepted them as true, not rejecting them on their face; similarly, if He noticed that sometimes his ('Usman's) prayers were not genuine or sincere, He should not throw them back in his face; instead, He should show some kindness and mercy and accept them.

Nizamuddin went on to narrate a miracle associated with Shaikh 'Usman and the dish available in his *deg* (cauldron). Once, a saintly *darwesh sahib-i-dil* came to him and ordered some food. Shaikh 'Usman put the large spoon, *kafgir*, inside the *deg*, and when he took it out, it was full of pearls (*durr wa marwarid*). The dervish refused, saying he had no use for them. Shaikh 'Usman put the *kafgir* in the *deg* again, bringing out pieces of gold this time. The dervish refused again, saying the previous ones (pearls) were stone-dust (*sang-rizeh*) and these (gold pieces) were stones (*sang*). That these were of no use to him. Bring out something that he could eat, he said. Shaikh 'Usman put the *kafgir* inside the *deg* for the third time and brought out the vegetables he had cooked. Seeing this miracle, the dervish advised 'Usman to leave the place as the miracles were to be hidden and not performed at will. Shaikh 'Usman died soon after. Now that the secrets of his close association with God were revealed (that is, his ability to perform miracles), there was no point in delaying meeting Him.[8]

It is recorded in the *Fawa'id-ul-Fu'ad* that the matter of whether offering food to people was a meritorious act or not came up for discussion at Hazrat Nizamuddin's hospice (*sukhan dar fazilat ita'am uftaad*). He said offering a meal to people was a noble act (*neeko cheez-ist ta'am be-khalq daadan*). The most striking story is its appreciation by the thirteenth-century Mongol conqueror, Chingiz Khan. The Mughal rulers of India traced their descent from their mother's side to him. Chingiz Khan, in turn, traced his ancestry to the mythical matriarch, Alanqua. Her dominating presence is well represented in Mughal painting.[9] Nizamuddin narrated an anecdote regarding the capture of Khwaja 'Ali, son of Shaikh Ruknuddin Chishti, during a raid by the Mongols, referred to as the infidel Tartars (*dar khuruj kuffar tatar*). Khwaja 'Ali was brought to the presence of Chingiz Khan. A disciple of the Sufi family was in the service of the great Khan and enjoyed a certain level of influence in his court. Seeing Khwaja 'Ali as a captive, he was disturbed. He thought about how he could get him released (*tariq khalas u chegune baashad*) and refer to him in front of Chingiz Khan. Eventually, after a lot of thought, he went to the Khan and submitted before him. He said that the captive, Khwaja 'Ali, should be released, as his father was a saintly figure and would often offer food to people (*pedar in mard mardi buzurg bud ta'am be-khalq dadi u ra khalas baayad dad*).

Chingiz Khan asked whether he fed his own people or strangers (*khalq khud ra ta'am dadi ya khalq bigane ra*)? The man replied, everyone feeds their own people, but his father used to distribute food among strangers. Impressed, Chingiz Khan said a person who offers food to God's creatures is very noble (*che nek kasi bud keh khalq khuda ra ta'am mi-dad*). He ordered that the prisoner be immediately released. He also apologized to Khwaja 'Ali and offered a robe (*khil'at*). Concluding the story, Nizamuddin remarked that offering food to people is a recommended practice in all religions (*ta'am dadand dar kul mazahib pasandideh ast*).[10]

Those who participated in the meritorious act

of commensality as eaters also thought that they were party to the merit, for they contributed to the process, as without them the noble act was not completed. A *darwesh sahib-i-dil* went to the religious head (*sadr-i-jahan*) of Bukhara (now in Uzbekistan) and sought the latter's intercession for a favour from the ruler of the place. The religious head tried to dismiss the dervish, saying he did not know him. The dervish told the religious head that he owed him an obligation (*ma ra bar tu haqqi ast*). The religious head asked, 'What obligation (*chi haq*)?' The dervish replied, 'Once you were sitting with food spread, and I came and joined in eating with you. So, I ate the food you served. This is the obligation.' That is, the head was rewarded for the meritorious act of feeding people, and the dervish helped him in being rewarded by eating what he served. Hearing this, the religious head went to the ruler and got the dervish's work done.[11]

Despite the Sufis insisting on moderation in conduct, there is a report of a large feast, lasting several days, which was organized by Shadi Khan and Khizr Khan, sons of Sultan Alauddin Khalji, to celebrate becoming disciples of Nizamuddin Auliya. Specific details of what was served in the feast are not clear, but Nizamuddin's earliest biographer,

Muhammad Jamal Qiwam, wrote about it within twenty-five years of the passing away of the saint with much enthusiasm and satisfaction.[12] Glimpses of food served in royal parties, imagined or real, can be seen in the near-contemporary Hindawi *premakhyana* texts, *Chandayan* (fourteenth century) of Mulla Da'ud and in *Padmavat* (sixteenth century) of Malik Muhammad Jayasi.

Madhu Trivedi has recently showed how Mulla Da'ud takes the readers of his *Chandayan* to a culinary journey into the fourteenth century, through a detailed list of cuisine prepared for royal feasts. Live animals (*sauj*) brought by the hunters, included deer, blue bulls, sambhar, antelopes, sheep and goats. A number of birds (*pankhi*) were also hunted, including quail, partridges and large black and white stork. These were slaughtered, cleaned and cooked in different ways, using a variety of spices, herbs and oil or ghee, and served fried or in gravy. As vegetarianism was on slow ascendance, some vegetable and the now-usual *paneer* dishes were also mentioned besides pickles and curd. These were served with different kinds of rice, which are named and identified by their flavour and aroma. A *kewra*-flavoured wheat was also referred to for making delicious bread.[13]

In his *Padmavat*, Malik Muhammd Jayasi had given more elaborate details of imaginatively conceived royal feasts, including the wedding party for the marriage of Ratan Sen and Padmavati and a feast organized by Ratan Sen in honour of Sultan Alauddin Khalji. Different kinds of *puris*, *chapatis* and rice were served with meat of a large number of animals, birds and fish – identified with their Awadhi–Hindi names. The most spectacular preparation and service must have been the whole goats (*chhagar*), dressed with aromatic spices, being put on spits and roasted. Different varieties of vegetarian dishes (*tarkari*) were also prepared, using pumpkins, gourds, brinjals, etc. Those looking for starters and side dishes such as *samosa, raita, mattha* (buttermilk) and *papaad* would not be disappointed either. A number of desserts like *petha*, made of white pumpkins roasted in ghee, served in mango syrup (*guramab*), were also mentioned. Typically, the traditional Indian *paan* (betel leaves) completed a delightful gastronomical extravaganza.[14]

From the point of view of Sufic prescriptions or ideals (*adab*), these could be considered unnecessary wastage of resources (*israf*). There were also concerns regarding the *halal* source of income, and whether animals were slaughtered through *halal* method (which requires slow cutting of the animal's nerves on the front side of the neck and bits of the neck also, rather than felling it with one big bang on the back of the animal's neck, separating the head from the body). Unamused, Kabir questioned the slaughter: *jori kari jibahi karen, kahte hain ja halal* (forcibly slaughter the animal, *zabah,* and call it *halal*). Violence against animals apart, feasting was also odd, as the Sufis were supposed to be enduring pain and sorrows. Prophetic ideals of poverty also made them proud *faqirs* and dervishes.

In conclusion, Hazrat Nizamuddin Auliya's discourses and other Sufi texts from medieval India provide considerable light on charitable endeavours, especially on feeding people, poor or not, and including arrangements for feeding the community (*langar*). At the same time, Sufis themselves were expected to eat minimally, avoiding non-vegetarian food in particular, for several reasons, including respecting the sentiments of large numbers of Hindu devotees. Already by the fifteenth century, beef-eating had emerged as a controversial issue, and any suspicion of mixing beef could be prevented by being publicly seen as not eating meat. Avoiding meat-eating also took care of sexual desires that were presumed to be caused by red meat. It is for this reason that pork was not recommended in Islam. Abstaining from eating meat also presumably helped maintain long hours of ritual purity, ablutions (*wuzu*), by checking air movements in the stomach. The capability to maintain long hours of ablution was also something to be marvelled at in Sufi circles.

After all, in attempting to reach near God, Sufis were to be seen as rising above the normal natural processes. Miracles, for instance, were explained as possible paranormal performance, *khirq-i-'adat*, that is, against the normal practice, which cannot be rationally explained. This was to be accepted as a reflection of God's power, *qudrat*. Sufis submitted to His will, including while eating or fasting. Fasting as an exercise in self-control was well-known, but eating only for God's sake was another dimension. These actions were understandable, but Sufis claiming to be doing everything for His sake could land them in trouble and give rise to suspicion and mistrust in the eyes of the *ulama*. These could include a Sufi mating with his wife and claiming it to be a virtuous act. Because this aspect of life creates difficulty in complete devotion for God – maintaining ritual purity, and siring children – Sufis tended to remain unmarried (*mujarrad*) and styled themselves as people wedded to God. This was, however, against the Prophet's advice on marriage and leading a good family life.

The Sufis were on safer terrain when they spoke about avoiding eating or fasting as part of spiritual exercises or about wholesome food served to visitors at Sufi hospices and feasting. There is also a striking contrast in the merits of less eating, or non-eating for many days of meditation (as in the case of Bibi Aliya) and the virtues of offering rich platters of large quantities of food to God's creatures (*khalq-i-khuda*), including humans and animals. These included a simple vegetarian rice preparation, *tahiri*, flavoured with some spices, herbs and dry fruits, and regularly served in *langar*. For Sufis who maintained poverty as a matter of pride, it was recommended that if nothing was immediately available, at least a glass of water could be served to guests. Nizamuddin narrated an anecdote where a Sufi felt helpless and embarrassed as he had nothing to offer to the early-morning visitors during an Eid festivity. What charisma could a Sufi display, if guests were not offered anything to eat? Sufis had the option to borrow money from neighbours or perform a miracle (*karamat*) to produce gold so that some provisions could be purchased for the family and guests. This was reported to be so for Khwaja

Qutbuddin Bakhtiyar Kaki (died 1235), successor of Muinuddin Chishti (died 1236) of Ajmer, in the Chishti Sufi order. Bakhtiyar Kaki produced gold coins for his wife to run the household. Delhi's Qutub Minar is named after this saint, whose shrine is not far from the historic thirteenth-century tower. The title *kaki* attached to his name means bread, which was said to be miraculously provided to serve his family. As a full-time Sufi, he did not earn anything, and the family normally ran on unasked-for gifts from followers.[15] The Sufis did struggle to maintain their families, though personally they were content to be the guests of God!

6

RESPECT FOR WOMEN

Ham ishq talab kuni o ham jaan khwahi
Har dow talabi wali muyassar na-shawad

You seek love and lust for the body
Simultaneously achieving both is not possible.

– Bibi Fatima Sam of Delhi, thirteenth century, quoted by Hazrat Nizamuddin Auliya, in *Fawa'id-ul-Fu'ad*

The *khanaqahs* and *dargahs* of Sufis have long been open for women to seek blessings and benediction. Despite patriarchal restrictions in society, some women have gone on to distinguish themselves in Sufism with charisma and power, which they used for the benefit of the people. Medieval Sufi literature – *malfuzat* and *tazkiras*, besides other genres – have for long referred to women in respectful terms. The literature includes *hikayats* and *karamats* attributed to saintly women, making them recognized in both popular perception and in Sufi fraternities as evolved and blessed souls in their own right.

The *dargahs* of some of them remain important centuries after their departure from this perishable world. Sufi tradition believes saints never die and that they continue to work for the general public welfare even as they lie resting in their graves (*mazars*). Thus, their *dargahs* attract a large number of people, especially on Thursday nights (*juma'rat*) and on the occasion of their *Urs*, that is, the death anniversary of the *buzurg* or saint buried there. Love for God and service to humanity remain central to all traditions of Sufism generally. These are conceptually articulated in Sufi traditions as *ishq-i-ilahi* (love for the divine), *tazkiya-i-nafs* (cleansing of the lower self) and *khidmat-i-khalq* (service and care for all the creations of God, which not only includes human beings, but also animals, plants and all objects). Sufis, as evolved human beings, are thus expected to represent what are identified as the best traditions of Islam in terms of grace and beauty of faith (*ihsan* and *iman*). Such persons are filled with thoughts of love for God and His creations.[1]

Majnun's madness for Laila epitomized the ideal of pain endured for seeking union with the beloved. An anecdote narrated by Nizamuddin illustrates this point further. Once, people were busy in a congregational prayer and Majnun disrupted the *namazis* by wandering into their midst. Finishing the *namaz* quickly, they surrounded and confronted Majnun, accusing him of acting like an uncultured infidel, or *kafir*. Majnun inquired what his fault was, if he had said anything. The crowd responded that he was blindly roaming around in front of the rows of *namazis* – a terrible violation of norms regarding proper conduct during prayers. Majnun responded that he was so engrossed in thoughts of Laila that he never noticed anyone praying while walking across the corridor, but what sort of lovers of God were they, that they were engaged in a conversation with Him and yet noticed his presence? Sufis thought Majnun was better than normal people in his undying devotion, and they were better than Majnun, as he wasted his life on a perishable Laila, whereas Sufis devoted themselves to their love for God, who was eternal.[2]

Some episodes from the lives of some such charismatic personalities from the Delhi Sultanate will illustrate how women were valued in their own times, celebrated as well as invoked in posterity.

Rabiya of Basra

Generations of Sufi figures were inspired by the extraordinary credentials of Rabiya of Basra in Iraq in her love for God (*ishq-i-Ilahi*), the principal obsession in the Sufi *tariqa* or path. Belonging to the early generation of the Sufis, five centuries before Nizamuddin, Rabiya Basri set the agenda by example of what it means to be a Sufi lover of God. Of the many stories relating to Rabiya, who was feared and respected for her iconoclasm, one is particularly instructive. Once she was rushing around with a bucket full of water in one hand and a bucket with fire in the other. When people stopped and inquired what she was doing, she told them that she was going to set paradise on fire and would also extinguish the hellfire. Through this, she was protesting that people worshipped God either out of fear of hell or for the rewards of heaven. Few people worshipped God just for the love of Him!

Alarmed by the cynical approach of the conservative custodians of religious practices, some of her followers feared that she would be punished by God for her deviance and disrespect for traditional norms of Islam. Fortunately for them, one of the disciples saw her in a dream after her death, to his assurance and to the satisfaction of the larger fraternity of devotional Islam of the Sufi kind, that Allah had forgiven all her acts of omission or commission, because she used to feed a stray dog outside her home every night.

Sufis have always been faced with the challenge of complete dependence on God to the extent that they would not seek help from Him for even a mere creature comforts. They would endure embarrassing poverty both as a test of their faith in all-knowing God's wisdom and as an excruciating sacrifice in their love for him. The advice in the Qur'an is not to plead for help from people, nor to turn down any request from them for some favour. The Prophet explained that those seeking help should not be humiliated, nor should any help be sought from people. If at all, one should seek help from the beneficent God. Elaborating on this, Ali Hujwiri, a scholar who authored the earliest treatise on Sufism in Persian, *Kashf al-Mahjub*, related an anecdote to the effect that a prosperous man (*ahl-i-duniya*) once told Rabiya that she could ask for any help from him whenever needed; he would give whatever she required (*chizi bekhwah az man ta muradat haasil kunam*). Surprised at the audacity of the man, Rabiya retorted: she was ashamed to ask for anything from God, the creator of the world; how could she shamelessly ask for help from God's creature – someone just like her (*sharm na daram keh az chun khwishtani khwaham*)?[3]

The Dargah of Bibi Fatima Sam

Several references to the spiritual excellence of Bibi Fatima Sam of thirteenth-century Delhi are recorded in Sufi discourses related to Nizamuddin Auliya and his successors in the Chishti *silsila*. Later, during the Mughal era, Shaikh Abdul Haq Muhaddis Dehlawi brought together some of the details from the life of Bibi Fatima in his *Akhbar-ul-Akhyar*, which is the finest collection of biographies of Indian Sufi figures from the Sultanate period onwards.[4]

Bibi Fatima Sam was like a sister to Shaikh Fariduddin Ganj-i-Shakar and his brother, Shaikh Najibuddin Mutawakkil. Nizamuddin Auliya is quoted by Abdul Haq Muhaddis as saying that, for Bibi Fatima Sam, feeding the poor was the most meritorious of all the pious activities. According to her, offering a loaf of bread with a glass of water in the name of God would accrue such blessings that were not possible to elicit even from lakhs of days of fasting and praying. This conformed with the Prophetic tradition, according to which people visiting Prophet Muhammad would not leave before eating things such as bread and dates. Even if the Prophet was known to have proclaimed, 'My poverty is my pride,' there was a lot of emphasis in early Islamic sources, particularly the Qur'an and *hadith*, on feeding the poor and the needy.[5]

Returning to Bibi Fatima Sam, whose *mazar* is located in a small but conspicuous tomb in Delhi, she was a formidable character and commanded a lot of respect in the Sufi circles of the thirteenth century. Her charitable endeavours, her reputation as someone who had performed the pilgrimage of *hajj* in Mecca, maintained the sanctity of ritual purification all her life. And her ability to dabble in extempore poetry was a source of her immense popularity.[6] Fatima Sam could definitely ward off fake devotees who pretended love for God while simultaneously seeking the pleasures of the body, a contradiction in terms:

Ham ishq talab kuni o ham jaan khwahi
Har dow talabi wali muyassar na-shawad

You seek love and lust for the body
Simultaneously achieving both is not possible.

Despite Fatima Sam's popularity, the fact that she was a woman was of concern to the patriarchal attitude of the time. Nizamuddin quoted his preceptor, Shaikh Fariduddin Ganj-i-Shakar, as saying that Fatima Sam was a man (*mard*) sent by God in the form of a woman (*zan*). Sufis believed that the excruciating pain endured by practitioners of the mystic path was an act of *mardanagi* (masculinity). This power of *mardanagi* transcended normal gendered differentiations. Nizamuddin explained that when a tiger comes out of the jungle people do not ask whether it was male or female. That is, the important thing is the sons of Adam are known for their respectable character, marked by devotion and piety (*ta'at-o-taqwa*).[7]

Karamat by Baba Farid's Mother

Fariduddin Ganj-i-Shakar had informed his disciples that his mother was known for her mystical attainments. Once, a thief broke into their house when all the members had retired for the night except for his mother, who was engrossed in her prayers. The moment the thief entered the house, he lost his sight. Unable to escape, the thief remarked that the inmates of the house were like his family members. It can be said with certainty that the terror created by the presence of whoever was in the house had blinded him (*az mahabat-i u kur shudam*). He sought forgiveness and intercession: 'Pray that my sight is restored. I repent and swear that I will not commit theft for the rest of my life'. On hearing the thief's invocations, the shaikh's mother prayed for the restoration of his sight. Having got his vision back, the thief left the house. His mother kept silent about the incident. Later in the morning, the thief returned along with his family, narrated the account of the previous night's encounter and converted to Islam at the hands of the shaikh's mother (*amadeh-am ba-ahl-i bait-i khwud ta musalman shawam*).[8]

Bibi Zulaikha's Blessings

Hazrat Nizamuddin Auliya used to refer to his mother, Bibi Zulaikha, as a saintly woman who was wholly dedicated in her devotion to God. Later in life, whenever Nizamuddin was in trouble, he would visit her grave in Delhi and seek her blessings, as he did during the struggle with Sultan Qutbuddin Mubarak Shah Khalji, who was continuously harassing him. Though the sultan's own close associate, Khusrau Khan, assassinated him, Nizamuddin believed he was eliminated due to his mother's curse. He had visited her grave immediately before the sultan's death and spoke of how the sultan harassed him. He prayed to his mother to help him settle the matter, or he would not be able to visit her grave again, as he feared he would be killed.[9]

Bibi Sarah

Bibi Sarah was a saintly mother of another early Sufi in Delhi, Shaikh Nizamuddin Abul Mu'ayyad. An anecdote narrated by Abdul Haq Muhaddis Dehlawi recounted a miracle at a time when Delhi was facing a long period of drought, and prayers for rain had had no effect. Nizamuddin took out a thread from the lower end of his mother's skirt (*daaman*) and waved it towards the sky and pleaded with God: this thread is from the skirt of this pious woman, who has remained protected from the gaze of a stranger (*na-mahram* – one who is not allowed to enter a woman's apartment in a purdah culture). Send rain on account of her chastity. Before the sentence was completed, it started raining.[10]

In the older version of this miracle, which was narrated by Nizamuddin Auliya, a piece of cloth from Bibi Sarah's skirt was used by her son in his prayers, though her name is not mentioned. A group of distressed people came to Shaikh Nizamuddin Abul Mu'ayyad and asked him to lead a congregational prayer for rain. Having agreed to give a sermon, the shaikh ascended the pulpit in front of a large gathering. The people noticed that he had stopped his speech to wave a piece of cloth to the sky, reciting something (which they could not hear). Soon, it started drizzling. The shaikh then got busy with his sermon. As the drizzle seemed to stop, the shaikh took out the cloth and waved again. This time, the rain came pouring down! On returning home, when inquired about the garment used by him, he replied that it was his mother's skirt.[11] Her grave is in Mehrauli, South Delhi, not far from the tomb of Khwaja Qutbuddin Bakhtiyar Kaki. The latter was the successor (*khalifa*) of Khwaja Moinuddin Sijzi Ajmeri, in the Chishti order of Sufism in medieval India.[12]

Bibi Aliya and Her Spiritual Dedication

In the section on female saintly personalities in his *Akhbar-ul-Akhyar*, Abdul Haq Muhaddis had also written a short biographical note on Bibi Aliya of Delhi. The despotic Sultan Muhammad bin Tughlaq was devoted to her. She was known for enduring all the excruciating pain in spiritual exercises, which only the most accomplished Sufis were known for practising. According to reports, she would shut herself in her inner chamber for *chilla*. During this period, she would only keep forty cloves with her for sustenance. When she would come out after completing the forty-day *chilla*, people would notice that she had eaten only a few cloves, and the rest of them would be lying there. Eating very little or not eating at all is a much-recommended act in Sufi discourses. Bibi Aliya had shown that it was possible and necessary to overpower hunger.[13]

These saintly women dedicated their lives in pursuit of ethical and moral conduct in Sufi spirituality, which brought them near to God. This, in turn, helped them acquire some paranormal powers, like the perceived ability to perform miracles (*karamat*), for which they became popular in their own life and in times to come. The blessed atmosphere of the Sufi *dargahs* guides people to become better human beings and also helps resolve their spiritual and material concerns with some mercy and kindness. These are particularly relevant in times of increasing intolerance, hate and violence in the name of religion.

It is possible to understand the anecdotes in Sufi literature from the vantage points of disciplinary practices of folklore studies, history of religion, literary history and gender and intersectionality. The stories involving women particularly highlight the powers of ethical and moral precepts stressed by those charismatic personalities; women who commanded respect in a society and fraternity that was clearly patriarchal and homosocial. The Sufis took a position that was different from the usual male dismissal of women as problematic, including maintaining ambiguities on the participation of women in *mahfil-i-sama*, musical assemblies. Anecdotes of the kind narrated above testify to the major presence of women in Sufi fraternities, sometimes performing miracles of the kind generally attributed to male saints. Some boundaries were certainly being broken.

As in most attempts at achieving excellence in Islamic societies, the practices of the Prophet were considered the ideal to follow. In this case, respect for women and appreciation of their excellence are reiterated in Sufi conversations and writings with reference to the Prophet. In the famous *hadith* on the relief and pleasure in *namaz*, the presence of wife Ayesha and daughter Fatima was discussed in detail in one of the assemblies of Nizamuddin Auliya. This was done with added emphasis on how noble men pray to God with reference to the extraordinary credentials of women around them. Men with several daughters were also considered to be blessed as God was supposed to have ensured that the latter were born with means for their bread and butter already arranged. Women were also continuously praised for their fine abilities.

Sufis have also struggled to deal with their relationship with women. As human beings, they needed to deal with bodily desires, for which they could marry a woman, which would mean maintaining a family and siring children, which would, in turn, be difficult to manage with self-inflicted poverty. Complete devotion and love for God would also mean a life spent in His service to the extent of neglecting the family, which is not an advisable proposition. The wife will expect both physical intimacy and material comfort. In Qur'anic terms, God advises men: wives are like a garment to you, and you are a garment for the wives. Thus, marriage was a recommended practice, but some Sufis wanted to remain bachelors (*mujarrad*). This would mean they were deprived of women companions with all their beautiful charm and excellent conduct.

The exemplar Prophet Muhammad was clear in his understanding. Marry women for benefiting from four virtuous reasons: their property, pedigree, beauty and faith (*maal*, *hasab*, *husn* and *din*). He especially recommended women with faith in Islam, as this would lead to the satisfaction of being in the company of an agreeable fellow believer. The man likes the company of such a wife; the faith of Islam is strengthened without discord, and both love each other. This was better than leading a lonely life and falling into the trap of a vicious Satan as company, which could lead to disgrace. Yet a man completely devoted to God and, therefore, remaining single can be better placed than those who carry the burden of maintaining a family.[14] A leading early Sufi, Hasan Basri, had humorously commented: light people got salvation, heavy ones were ruined (*naja al-mukhiffuna wa halaka al-muthqiluna*).[15]

On what pious women themselves thought was good for them, it will be appropriate to refer to a fine treatise on Sufism by a female Sufi, A'ishah al-Ba'uniyyah (died 1517), of Damascus, Syria. *The Principles of Sufism* is an authoritative and elegant guide to Sufism by a female Sufi master. The book was originally written in Arabic: *Al-Muntakhab fi usul al-rutab fi 'ilm al-tasawwuf* (Selections on the Principles of the Stations in the Science of Sufism). In short, *The Principles of Sufism* emphasize repentance (*tauba*), sincerity (*ikhlas*), remembrance (*zikr*) and love (*muhabbat*) as key elements in the Sufi path for mystical union with God – these are the central features of Sufism worldwide. The author has drawn on important and interesting insights from selections of teachings and anecdotes from the Qur'an, traditions relating to the Prophet, and the lives of Sufi masters of previous generations. Daughter of the chief judge of Damascus – Shafi'i jurist Yusuf al-Ba'uni (died 1475), whose family was related to an important branch of Qadiri *silsila* – A'ishah was trained as a Sufi master in her own right and was much respected for not only her mystical compositions, but also for her piety and charisma.[16] That a woman mystic could express her spiritual experiences in writing and command respect as an accomplished Sufi practitioner and scholar in the fifteenth and early-sixteenth centuries once again indicates the value of the graceful and charismatic presence of women in Sufi fraternities historically.

The gates of the hospices of Sufi shaikhs, such as that of Nizamuddin Auliya, were open for everyone, and women were not barred from his presence. They were as entitled to partake in spiritual conversations and poetry as men and other gendered beings were. Patriarchal discriminations apart, the circle of the Sufis showed a remarkable acceptance of women in their midst. Persian Sufi poetry was certainly aimed at transcending all differences. Much of it was about love, pain and sorrows attached with it. Nizamuddin Auliya liked to quote one such couplet:

Bar 'ishq tu wa bar tu nazar khwaham kard
Jaan dar gham-i tu zer-o-zabar khwaham kard

I will look at you and your love
I will destroy myself in your sorrow.[17]

7

MIRACLE AS A SOURCE OF BENEVOLENCE

> There are four kinds of miracles: *mu'jizaat* (prophetic marvels), *karamaat* (miracles of Sufis), *istidraj* (extraordinary feats of non-Muslim holy-men), and *ma'unat* (illegitimate trickery). Matters beyond rational understanding pertain to the realm of miracles. Magic (*jadu*) and evil eye (*nazar*) are equally possible.
>
> – Hazrat Nizamuddin Auliya on popular beliefs, as quoted in *Fawa'id-ul-Fu'ad*

This chapter will discuss Sufi miracles (*karamat*) as a source of benevolence, throwing light on a fascinating aspect of Sufis' personalities. The reports of the Sufis' interventions for the larger public good made them authoritative figures in society, and people turned to them when in need. The Sufi shaikhs' bestowal of kingship to deserving candidates as future rulers, their significant roles as spiritual healers, prevention of natural calamities, protection from enemies and ensuring the safety of merchants and pilgrims during travels, etc., contributed to their popularity as well as claims to their authority in society. In view of the abundance of material in Sufi literature, including anecdotes narrated by Hazrat Nizamuddin Auliya, the chapter will focus on miracles performed by Sufi saints, especially when it came to Sufi healing practices.

Belief in the evil eye and magic is popular in many religions and cultures. The Chishti Sufi shaikhs and their followers were no exception. Hazrat Nizamuddin and his *khalifa* Nasiruddin Chiragh-i-Dehli firmly believed that the evil eye (*nazar*) and black magic (*jadu*) had the power to destroy their target. Hazrat Nizamuddin would even criticize the rationalist sect of Mu'tazalites for their refusal to believe in it.[1] In Nasiruddin Chiragh-i-Dehli conversations, *Khair-ul-Majalis*, it is recorded that the illness of Prophet Muhammad, Shaikh Fariduddin and some others were due to the effect of black magic. Nasiruddin also narrated the story of a bag being found, which contained an idol made of flour with many needles inserted in different parts of it. The idol was believed to be responsible for a serious illness of Shaikh Fariduddin, who was cured only after it was destroyed.[2]

Visits to the tombs of the Sufi shaikhs, their relics and amulets (*ta'wiz*) distributed by them were considered effective healing means. According to an anecdote in *Fawa'id-ul-Fu'ad*, a large number of visitors came to Shaikh Fariduddin's hospice to collect amulets and Hazrat Nizamuddin, then a young disciple, was tired of preparing them.[3] Hazrat Nizamuddin's ailing mother also once asked him to visit the grave of martyrs (*shahids*) and holy men (*buzurg*). Her condition reportedly improved when he visited the graves and prayed for her health. In another anecdote, an ailing Shaikh Fariduddin sent Nizamuddin and some other disciples to the graves of martyrs in the area to pray for his health. References in the texts clearly show that both the Sufis and the regular people believed in the theory that the saints never die, and while resting in the grave, they continued to perform the social function the way they did while alive.[4]

Referring to the death of saints and their spiritual state after death, Hazrat Nizamuddin recounted the following story. He had a friend in Badaun whose name was Ahmad. He was very upright and pious and had qualities like those of the men of the invisible world, the spiritual dimension (*abdaal*). Though he was illiterate, he had devoted himself to understanding juristical issues and their implementation. When Nizamuddin moved to Delhi, Ahmad also settled there. One day, they happened to meet on the road. As soon as Ahmad saw Nizamuddin, he began asking him questions about various legal problems. Then he inquired about the health of Nizamuddin's mother. Ahmad already knew about her illness but had not known that she had passed away. Nizamuddin informed Ahmad that she had been blessed with God's mercy; she had died. May you live a long life, was his rejoinder. Sometime later, Ahmad also departed from this world. One night, Nizamuddin saw him in a dream. Just as he would during his lifetime, he began asking him questions about the law and its application. Why are you asking me about this now, Nizamuddin asked, suggesting that while he was alive, that was a commendable vocation, but surely not after death? Ahmad replied, 'Do you really think that the saints of God are dead?'[5]

Later, Amir Khwurd records that a large number

of devotees would flock to the *dargah* of Khwaja Qutbuddin Bakhtiyar Kaki even in the days of Hazrat Nizamuddin, and the former knew about people visiting him.[6] It is from this perspective that one can appreciate the reason for the quarrel amongst people over the dead body of a Sufi shaikh. In one case of Abdullah Ansari, a tenth-century Sufi saint and poet, it was announced that the different groups of claimants would come one by one, lift his body and carry him away to their particular graveyard. All tried, but failed, except the Sufis who lifted the body and appropriated him. Ansari is known in history as a Sufi.[7]

Apart from the manufactured *ta'wiz*, relics, tombs and tanks for ritual bathing, which were known for their healing powers,[8] there were some other methods in alternative medicine. For example, a disciple of Shaikh Fariduddin was suffering from a serious backache. The shaikh called the disciple and asked him to bend forward and placed his hands on the disciple's waist. Surprisingly, the pain disappeared.[9] This ability of the shaikh to cure a patient is further testified by Hazrat Nizamuddin Auliya's statement on the value of ta'wiz and sacral 'touching' of the shaikh. It is related that once Shaikh Fariduddin asked his preceptor, Khwaja

Qutbuddin Bakhtiyar Kaki, about what he should do when people approached him requesting amulets. 'This work,' replied Khwaja Bakhtiyar Kaki, 'rests neither in your hand nor in mine. The amulet has God's name inscribed on it; write and give them God's word.' Nizamuddin further said that when he was an apprentice at Shaikh Fariduddin's hospice, it occurred to him many times that at an opportune moment he should ask Shaikh Fariduddin for permission to write amulets. Once, Badruddin Ishaq, who usually assisted in writing amulets, was not present, and Shaikh Fariduddin asked Nizamuddin to write the amulets instead. As the crowd was huge, he wrote many and was soon overwhelmed by requests. At one point, Shaikh Fariduddin asked Nizamuddin whether he was getting tired. Nizamuddin replied that the spiritual boon of the master was present and sustaining him. After that, Shaikh Farid authorized Nizamuddin to write and give amulets on his own, adding that anything touched by the hands of saints produces a healing effect (*masase daste buzurgaan ham kari daarad*).[10]

Together with this 'divine touch', 'blowing' or 'breathing' (*jhaar-phunk* in Hindi) was also an important source of healing. Implicit in it was the belief that some kind of *jinn* (demon) was behind the sickness of a person. The Sufi shaikhs, owing to their spiritual knowledge and power, were capable of dealing with these demons to provide relief to the sick.[11] Apart from healing the sick, there are also cases of Sufi shaikhs reviving the dead. In one account, the performance of this miracle by Khwaja Qutbuddin Bakhtiyar Kaki led to the conversion of thousands of non-Muslims to Islam. The Sufi shaikh's protection of the people and healing practices brought him immense popularity. Besides, the Sufi's healing power also came in handy to silence the opponents from amongst the *ulama*. According to an early report, Maulana Badruddin Hujjat Multani became a disciple after Hazrat Nizamuddin cured his eyes by placing his saliva into them. Another opponent, the qazi of Gopalpur, became a disciple after Nizamuddin saved him when his Arabia-bound ship dashed against a rock and shattered into pieces. Even a *qazi* of the Sultanate Army became a disciple after he was rescued by the saint in the neighbourhood of Multan. The last two anecdotes reveal that the Sufi shaikh's power extended beyond the boundary of his *wilayat* and his followers actually believed that the saint had the ability to transcend the limits of time and space.[12] The belief was given recognition by Hazrat

Nizamuddin himself when he told his audience (as recorded by Amir Hasan Sijzi) that a true dervish was a person who extricated himself from the clutches of time and place (*darwesh aan baashad keh az zaman o makaan bairun rafte baashad*).[13]

Referring to distinctive 'times', Hazrat Nizamuddin noted that some 'times' were distinguished from others. The festival day, for instance, is set apart from other days as a day of general celebration. Similarly, there may be a place in which one can find comfort, such as is available nowhere else. But a dervish should be the kind of person who has gone beyond the consideration of time or place. He should not be uplifted by any sense of joy or be depressed by sorrow. He should be the sort of person who has gone beyond the domain of this world, so much so that when he speaks, his heart remains focused on God; his tongue should be the instrument of his heart, and his heart the instrument of God. Further, Sufis can occasionally fail, for God may have decided so. While referring to the miraculous healing power of a relic of Shaikh Farid (a hair fallen from his beard), Hazrat Nizamuddin informed his audience that once a friend called Tajuddin Minai came to him and asked for the relic for his ailing child. The relic was not where it was usually kept. When all efforts to find the relic went in vain, Tajuddin Minai had to return home disappointed. His son died soon after. After some time, someone else asked for the relic, which was found at its usual place. Hazrat Nizamuddin concluded that the son of his friend was destined to die, and the relic had disappeared by itself.[14]

In all such cases, the relationship between the Sufi shaikhs and the followers was seen in terms of mutual fidelity and aid. The people venerated a Sufi and, in return, were blessed with patronage and protection. The people of Delhi protested against Khwaja Muinuddin Chishti's decision to take his disciple Khwaja Bakhtiyar Kaki from Delhi to Ajmer. The saint was moved by the public outcry and allowed his disciple to stay in Delhi. Shaikh Farid left Delhi because the people of his hometown, Hansi, did not have free access to him in the capital city. While the shaikh was living in Khwaja Bakhtiyar Kaki's house, a man from Hansi came to see him. He came to the house two or three times, and each time the doorkeeper denied him entry into the house. One day, as Farid was leaving the house, the man fell at his feet and began to sob. Why are you crying, asked the shaikh. 'Because,' replied the man, 'while you were at Hansi, I could see you easily, but now when I come to see you, it is very difficult.' That same day, Farid said to his friends that he was going to return to Hansi. Later, on relocating to Ajodhan, he was rebuked by a disciple for trying to keep aloof from the people.[15]

Hazrat Nizamuddin was asked by an unknown visitor to his hospice to stay in Ghiyaspur, his dwelling place in Delhi, when the saint was contemplating moving to a secluded place away from the crowd. Nizamuddin himself narrated this to his audience. The man, possibly belonging to the world of the unseen (*aalam-i-ghayb*), told him at the outset that he should not have become popular. Now that he has, he must work in a way that tomorrow, on the day of judgement, he should not feel ashamed in the presence of the Prophet (Muhammad). The man asked Nizamuddin: 'What power, what gain is there in retreating from people and immersing yourself in prayers?' When he finished speaking, Nizamuddin offered him some food, but the visitor did not eat it. It was only when the saint decided to continue residing in his hospice at Ghiyaspur that he took some food and left. Nizamuddin never saw him again.[16]

Later, when Nasiruddin Chiragh-i-Dehli expressed his desire to leave Delhi and settle in a faraway place, Hazrat Nizamuddin commanded him to stay in the city and work among the people. Subsequently, the murderous attack by a *qalandar* on Nasiruddin Chiragh shocked the populace in Delhi. Some people went to the extent of deciding that they would stone the *qalandar* to death. These and many other references in the Sufi texts show that the people of various towns and cities wanted the Sufis to stay in their neighbourhood and protect them in times of trouble. The departure of a Sufi from a particular area was considered a bad omen, a bolt from the blue. Hazrat Nizamuddin believed that the region of Punjab was protected from the thirteenth-century Mongol onslaught because of the presence of Shaikh Farid. In the year when Farid departed from this world, the Mongols invaded and devastated the region.[17] The fourteenth-century poet and historian, Izzuddin Isami, believed that Delhi was destroyed by Muhammad Tughlaq because God had removed Hazrat Nizamuddin from there. According to him, the monarchs were the head of the state, but it was the dervishes who averted the calamities. Had there been no saints, the world would not have continued to exist. The earth functions by the blessings of the saints.[18]

In conclusion, the Sufi shaikhs were often approached by people for curing various kinds of physical illness, recovery from body aches and even revival of the dead with the help of charms and amulets as well as through 'blowing' and 'touching'. Prevention of natural calamities such as drought and famine, protection from enemies and ensuring safe journey of merchants and pilgrims were also important functions expected from the Sufi shaikhs. The popularity of particular Sufis depended on how successfully they demonstrated their miraculous powers. The people appropriated a miracle-working Sufi shaikh, expected him to stay in their neighbourhood and perform miracles for them. The popularity of someone like Nizamuddin Auliya was not necessarily due to any organized propaganda by important disciples such as Amir Khusrau, Amir Hasan and Ziyauddin Barani, nor entirely due to a lavish distribution of cash and commodities among the poor and destitute by the saint, as was alleged by some of the opponents. Yet charity mattered, especially the public kitchen (*langar*), which provided for feeding the people. Hazrat Nizamuddin had a widespread following among the aristocracy as well, including the courtiers and members of the royal family, often for blessings and *tabarrukat* (sacred things). Miracles were a source of benevolence, which in turn made Sufis respected figures in society.

8

ENCOUNTERS WITH OPPONENTS

I have two doors in my house. If the sultan enters from one, I will vacate from the other.

– Hazrat Nizamuddin Auliya on Sultan Alauddin Khalji, threatening to come and forcibly meet him, as quoted in *Fawa'id-ul-Fu'ad*

The emergence of Sufi shaikhs from the seclusion of their hospices, with their authoritative position in society, was often contested by their opponents and people envious of the power they wielded. These included Sufis of rival orders, the *ulama*, contemporary rulers and leaders from other religious traditions. Often, rival claims to authority were settled through the performance of miracles. A large number of anecdotes in Sufi texts refer to the opposition, disrespect and abusive epithets of the sultans, *ulama* and other people of worldly influence, leading to the provocation of the wrath of the Sufis. It was believed that the Sufis' curse caused sudden and painful death of the opponents. For instance, it was reported that Shaikh Fariduddin Ganj-i-Shakar's curse led to the death of several of his opponents, including the administrator of Multan and the *qazi* of Ajodhan, in Punjab, who bore grudges against the Sufi shaikh and were conspiring to kill him.[1]

In some cases, the Sufi shaikhs left the issue to be decided by God and went to the extent of leaving the place, avoiding any violent confrontation. Khwaja Muinuddin Chishti wanted to take his successor, Khwaja Qutbuddin Bakhtiyar Kaki, from Delhi to Ajmer to avoid a conflict with the capital's leading religious authority, Shaikhul Islam Najmuddin Sughra. However, Bakhtiyar Kaki had to remain in Delhi due to a tremendous public and political demand, including the direct intervention and request by the contemporary Sultan Shamsuddin Iltutmish (ruled 1211–36).[2] Similarly, Hazrat Nizamuddin had to leave for Ajodhan to avoid meeting Sultan Jalaluddin Firuz Khalji.[3] Later, he remarked that he would leave the place if Jalaluddin's successor,

Sultan Alauddin Khalji, continued to bother him. The account reveals that the sultan's hostility came to an end only after Nizamuddin Auliya announced in no uncertain terms that he was not interested in matters of the government and would prefer to pray for the welfare of the people and their king, that is, Sultan Alauddin Khalji.[4] Contemporary Sufi literature also relates the subsequent faith of the sultan in the miraculous powers of Nizamuddin Auliya and Alauddin Khilji's sons, Khizr Khan and Shadi, joining as his disciples.[5] There are also reports in which the opponent was forgiven altogether. For example, Sultan Muhammad Tughluq did not face the wrath of Nasiruddin Chiragh-i-Dehli, despite his hostility towards the Sufi shaikhs the latter, in particular.[6]

What was the source of this conflict? The *wilayat* of the Sufi shaikh encroached, for all practical purposes, on the territorial authority of the ruler. If a major Sufi saint laid claims to spiritual rule over a territory, which the ruler held by force and ordered through the civil administration, then it was below the dignity of the Sufi to be seen under the ruler's protection and patronage. The Sufis should not be seen as accepting grants from the rulers and attending their courts. Conversely, they were not expected to entertain the rulers at their own hospices as well. In either case, there were difficulties with regard to power, protocols and etiquette. The rulers used their military power to announce their claims to authority in a territory in which the Sufis also exercised their own spiritual power. The Sufi shaikh's ability to bestow kingship, his role as protector of the people in times of crisis and his role as the healer of the sick brought tremendous popular following and support to him. Of particular note is the Sufis' massive following among the court officials and the soldiers.[7]

Thus, Nizamuddin's indifference towards the rituals of the sultan's *darbar,* his refusal to allow the reigning sultan to visit his hospice and his encroachment into the power base of the sultan, that is, with court officials and ordinary soldiers, constituted a threat to the political authority. In the conflict that followed, the official *ulama* sided with the sultan and raised the question of violation of the *shari'at* by Nizamuddin in such matters as listening to music and refusal to perform congregational prayers. The Sufi, in turn, looked down upon the theologians, condemned them as inhabitants of hell (*ahl-i-dozakh*). In most of these confrontations, Nizamuddin and his fellow Sufis are shown to have come out victorious, sometimes by establishing their superior knowledge of Islamic law, on other occasions by their healing and other miraculous abilities and on yet others by cursing the opponents to death. The message which came out from the Sufi circle was loud and clear: those provoking the Sufi shaikhs would be eliminated by the powers of their righteousness and miracles.

It is not possible to recount here all the episodes of encounters between Sufi shaikhs and the political authority, which are narrated in detail in Sufi texts. Hazrat Nizamuddin Auliya's defence of music at Ghiyasuddin Tughluq's court is analysed in detail in the next chapter. In this chapter, Nizamuddin's difficulties with Sultan Qutbuddin Mubarak Shah Khalji will be discussed in some detail.

Nearly two centuries later, Shaikh Jamali brought together in his *Siyar-ul-Arifin* all the reports of the conflict between Nizamuddin and the sultan. Shaikh Jamali, quoting Shaikh Nasiruddin Chiragh-i-Dehli, mentioned that after the death of Sultan Alauddin Khalji, Qutbuddin Mubarak Shah became the sultan by killing his brother Khizr Khan. Since Khizr Khan was a disciple of Nizamuddin Auliya, the new sultan began to doubt the saint's intentions. He could see that large numbers of the sultan's nobles and soldiers were disciples and followers of the Sufi shaikh. The earliest reference to the trouble is found in *Qiwam-ul-Aqa'id,* composed in Deccan within twenty-five years of Nizamuddin's passing away. It is related that Sultan Qutbuddin Mubarak Shah Khalji had summoned the eminent Sufi saint, Shaikh Ruknuddin Suhrawardi from Multan. When Shaikh Ruknuddin arrived in the court, the sultan told him that he had come all the way from Multan, but there was a person who stayed outside the wall of the fort and was indifferent towards his affairs. Shaikh Ruknuddin, despite being a Suhrwardi Sufi, had a lot of respect for his Chishti contemporary Hazrat Nizamuddin. He asked the sultan to refrain from making any statement against the great shaikh. He went on to give an appreciative lecture on Nizamuddin's high spiritual attainments. The sultan felt humiliated and withdrew his remarks against the saint, saying he bore no grudges against him and was only referring to reports of some people.[8]

Thus, the sultan was unable to get support from a leading Suhrawardi saint by trying to pit him against the Chishti Sufi, Nizamuddin, wanting to exploit any possible tension or rivalry between the Sufis of the two influential Sufi lineages or *silsila*. The author of *Qiwam-ul-Aqa'id,* Muhammad Jamal, had recorded that Sultan Qutbuddin continued with the hostility. Once, the sultan was drunk and had ordered the nobleman, Malik Talbugha Bughda, to remove his cap, which was gifted to him by Hazrat Nizamuddin. The malik, who was a disciple of Nizamuddin, did not obey the sultan's command. Enraged, the sultan took out his sword and shouted: 'Remove your cap or else your head will be cut off.' The malik replied that he cannot remove this cap of the shaikh for the sake of his life; the sultan may kill him if he so wishes. Astonished, the ruler let the malik go.[9]

It is recorded in the collection of Nasiruddin Chiragh-i-Dehli's discourse, *Khair-ul-Majalis*, that an opponent told the sultan that Nizamuddin refused to accept any gift from the sultan, while those offered by his nobles were accepted, despite the fact that the gifts presented by the nobles were actually from him. The sultan believed this report and ordered the officials to abstain from visiting the Sufi shaikh. Spies were stationed to report if any officer violated the order and to investigate how the shaikh ran his public kitchen in the absence of gifts from the nobles. When Nizamuddin learnt about this, he instructed his servant, Iqbal, to increase the quantity of the food cooked. He also directed Iqbal to pick up coins from a shelf in the hospice by just uttering *bismillah* (in the name of Allah). This miraculously doubled the coins. The sultan was accordingly informed that the shaikh's hospice was flourishing and the quantity of food prepared and served to the people had been doubled. The sultan felt humiliated and confessed to his associates that he was misguided and that the affairs of the shaikh pertained to the world of the unseen (*alam-i-ghaib*).[10]

Amir Khwurd Kirmani has mentioned in his *Siyar-ul-Auliya* that Sultan Qutbuddin was hostile towards Hazrat Nizamuddin for two reasons. Firstly, the sultan had built a congregational mosque at his capital, Siri. On the first Friday, after its completion, he had invited all the Sufis and *ulama* to offer prayers there. Nizamuddin had replied that there was a mosque near his place and that it was more appropriate that he should offer his prayers there. This response was not liked by the sultan. Secondly, it had become a custom that the Sufis, *ulama* and other notables of the city gathered at the sultan's court on the first day of the month and offered their greetings to the sultan. Nizamuddin avoided attending this party, but sent his servant Iqbal to represent him. This afforded an opportunity for the envious to provoke trouble. They reminded the ruler that Nizamuddin did not attend the congregational prayer in his mosque, nor did he come to greet him on the first day of the month; instead, he sent a slave to the court. Sufficiently provoked, the young sultan declared that if Nizamuddin did not come on the first day of the next month, he would have him brought forcibly.[11]

This remark of the sultan was brought to the notice of Hazrat Nizamuddin. He left for the tomb of his mother and stated that the sultan was contemplating harming him. If before the end of the month, 'his business was not settled', he would not be able to visit her in future. As the first of the month drew near, Nizamuddin's followers became increasingly concerned. The Sufi shaikh, however, derived assurance from his submission of the matter to his mother and sat waiting for whatever was going to happen. On the last night before the beginning of the new month, the sultan's closest associate, Khusrau Khan, rebelled and treacherously cut off his head, throwing his body down from the roof of the palace and setting the head on top of a lance, and announced himself as the new sultan of Delhi.[12] Nizamuddin was thus saved from the humiliation of attending Qutbuddin's monthly parties held on the pretext of sighting the new moon.

Later, the sultan sent a messenger to Nizamuddin and informed him that Shaikh Ruknuddin Suhrawardi was arriving from Multan to visit the court. Nizamuddin was also ordered to come: 'The shaikh lives in my territory, but never comes to meet me; it is essential that he visits the court this week.' Nizamuddin replied that he had never gone out, and that it was the custom of his Chishti preceptors (*pirs*) not to keep company with rulers and ministers, and requested that he be allowed to live in peace. The arrogant sultan disliked the shaikh's response and insisted that his order be followed. The shaikh, in turn, sent a messenger to the Suhrawardi Sufi shaikh, Ziyauddin Rumi, who was the spiritual guide of Sultan Qutbuddin, asking him to prevent his disciple from harassing him: 'Ask the sultan to refrain from taking up a fight with the dervishes.' Ziyauddin Rumi was on his deathbed at the time, so he could not do anything about it. He died two or three days later. The sultan and the religious leaders of the city had gathered at the grave of Ziyauddin Rumi for prayers (*fatiha*) on the third day after his death. When Hazrat Nizamuddin reached there, everyone rushed to greet him, but the sultan was jealously watching him from a distance. Some notables suggested to the shaikh to greet the sultan. The shaikh politely replied that the sultan was reciting the Qur'an and it was not proper to disturb him at this time.[13]

After the prayers, the sultan called the *ulama* for a meeting and asked them to convince Shaikh Nizamuddin of the necessity to visit him at the court once a week or at least on the first of every month. He ordered to be informed whether the shaikh had rejected the proposal so that he could take necessary action. Soon, a delegation of the leading *ulama* and Sufis arrived at Nizamuddin's hospice at Ghiyaspur and gave him the sultan's message. They pleaded that the shaikh should visit the court so that a conflict with the young and proud sultan could be avoided. The shaikh gave some thought to the advice and remarked: 'Let us see what turns out!'

Seeking to minimize the possibility of violence, the delegation returned to inform the sultan that the shaikh had agreed to the proposal to visit the court on the first of every month. On the twenty-seventh of the current month (of Shawwal), two court officials who were also disciples of the shaikh went to inquire whether the shaikh had actually decided to visit the court. The latter replied that he could not break the tradition of his Chishti preceptors, so there was no question of visiting the court.[14]

Thinking that the sultan was eagerly waiting for the first of the month, the non-arrival of the shaikh at the court may provoke trouble all around, the two disciples suggested that the shaikh should invoke his preceptor, Shaikh Fariduddin Ganj-i-Shakar's spiritual help, so that the tension dies down. The shaikh responded that he was ashamed of turning to his preceptor for such a small matter, adding that the sultan's defeat was imminent. He was assured of his victory as it was revealed to him in a dream the previous night that he was sitting on a high platform facing the *qibla* (that is, Ka'ba in Mecca in Arabia). In the meantime, an enraged bull appeared there and tried to attack him. He immediately got up, took the bull by its horns and brought it down to the floor. The wild creature died the very moment. As it turned out, Khusrau Khan attacked the sultan with the help of some of his supporters on the fateful day and killed him.[15]

Many of these episodes, such as the sultan's hostility towards Hazrat Nizamuddin, Shaikh Ruknuddin Suhrawardi's visit to Delhi at the invitation of the sultan and Khusrau Khan's rebellion and execution of the sultan, are also narrated by Ziyauddin Barani in his *Tarikh-i-Firuz Shahi*.[16] Barani was a contemporary political ideologue, historian, friend of Amir Khusrau and disciple of Nizamuddin Auliya.

In conclusion, it may be noted that the anecdotes in the two early texts, that is, Muhammad Jamal Qiwam's *Qiwam-ul-Aqa'id* and Nasiruddin Chiragh-i-Dehli's discourses, *Khair-ul-Majalis*, mention Sultan Qutbuddin Mubarak Shah Khalji's hostility towards Hazrat Nizamuddin Auliya, but do not refer to the latter's curse as the cause of his brutal death. It is in a slightly later text, Amir Khwurd Kirmani's *Siyar-ul-Auliya*, that the sultan is reported to have died on account of his hostility towards Hazrat Nizamuddin. Although Nizamuddin was confident of his victory, he had refrained from openly prophesying the death of the sultan before the first of the month, leading to rumours and speculations. The long narrative in Shaikh Jamali's *Siyar-ul-Arifin* brings together all the different strands concerning the conflict between the Sufi and the sultan. Here, the Sufi circle was assured of Nizamuddin's victory beforehand.

The anecdotes also point to the Suhrawardi connection in the conflict between the sultan and the shaikh. The sultan wanted to check Nizamuddin's powers by summoning Shaikh Ruknuddin Suhrawardi from Multan. The Suhrawardi shaikh was, however, wise enough to recognize Nizamuddin's spiritual authority and advised the sultan to refrain from provoking him. The anecdote in *Siyar-ul-Arifin* adds that Hazrat Nizamuddin had to send a messenger to Shaikh Ziyauddin Rumi Suhrawardi, said to be a spiritual guide of Sultan Qutbuddin, asking him to prevent his disciple from meddling in the affairs of the Chishti *silsila*. Nizamuddin and his successors continued to face difficulties at the hands of the rulers, who were often supported by rivals, especially theologians. Hazrat Nizamuddin's conflict with Sultan Ghiyasuddin Tughluq, who had forced the former to visit his court to establish Sufi music as a legitimate Islamic practice, had turned ugly. The acrimonious episode will be discussed in the next chapter.

9

DEFENCE OF SUFI MUSIC

Ishq ra bu hanifa dars na-guft
Shafi'i ra dar riwayat nist

Abu Hanifa did not teach lessons of love
Shafi'i is also not reported to have done so.

– Hazrat Nizamuddin Aulilya, as quoted in *Fawa'id-ul-Fu'ad*

In continuation with several ethical precepts and spiritual practices, Sufi music is about love for God and care for all his creations. Struggles over Sufi music and dance have a long history, with artists and connoisseurs running into difficulties with the custodians of public morality backed by political regimes. Yet for all their powers, they have not been able to suppress the artists and art forms forever. This chapter is on the troubles faced by Hazrat Nizamuddin Auliya on account of his interest in *qawwali*. Though there might have been other political issues behind the harassment, he was called for a judicial interrogation (*mahzar*) at Sultan Ghiyasuddin Tughluq's *darbar* to defend his interest in Sufi music, *sama* and *qawwali,* in the light of the *shari'at* or Sunni–Hanafi interpretation of Islam presented as law. Nizamuddin Auliya's arguments more or less settled the issue of the legitimacy of Sufi music as a popular and devotional art form, though naysayers have continued with their tirade. Some even attack Sufi practices in general.[1]

According to Amir Khwurd Kirmani, the author of the mid-fourteenth-century Sufi text, *Siyar-ul-Auliya,* Hazrat Nizamuddin identified four kinds of musical practice: *halal* (lawful), *haram* (forbidden), *makruh* (abominable) and *mubah* (permissible). If the connoisseur *(sahib-i wajd o haal)* is fairly attracted towards the divine, then his practise of *sama* is *mubah;* if he is inclined more towards *majaz* (worldly concerns), then it is *makruh;* if his interest is entirely for *majaz,* then it is *haram* and if he is fully devoted to God, *sama* is *halal* for him. The practitioner of music (*sahib-i sama)* should be capable of understanding these distinctions.[2]

Amir Khwurd further wrote, quoting from Nizamuddin's remarks (recorded in *Fawa'id-ul-Fu'ad),* that the singer *(musma)* should be an adult male, and not a boy or woman. The heart of the listener (*mustame)* should be full of love and devotion for God. The content (*masmu)* should not be vulgar (*fahash, hazl*). Musical instruments (*ala-i sama*) such as *chang* and *rabab* should not be used in *majlis-i-sama.*[3] Nizamuddin emphasized during his conversations with disciples that whatever was being heard was for remembering God (*yaad-i-haqq*) and, thus, it was a valid (*halal*) act.[4] Nizamuddin is also reported to have outlined the *adab* (norms) for *sama:* it should be held at an appropriate time when the heart is free from any anxiety; it should be organized at a place where the environment is soul-refreshing; the participants should belong to the same group of male adults known for their addiction *(zauq)* for *sama,* which in practise was a blend of poetry, music and dance. At the time of settling down in the *majlis* (musical assembly), one should wear a neat and perfumed attire.[5]

The above norms are supplemented with suggestions made by Fakhruddin Zarradi, a *khalifa* (spiritual successor) of Nizamuddin Auliya, who actively participated in the discussion on the legitimacy of Sufi music. According to Zarradi, *sama* should be listened to with full attention. The participants of the *majlis* should not look at each other or be conscious of each other's presence. Clearing one's throat and yawning should be avoided. The heads should be lowered and completely lost in contemplation. There should not be any movement of the body and one should keep one's *nafs* (the sensual aspect of one's being) in control so that dancing and clapping are avoided. However, if one is so lost or moved while listening to music that one suddenly starts crying, shaking or dancing, and the intention is not marred by any sense of ostentation or hypocrisy, then the actions will be treated as *mubah*. For, crying and wailing drown one's sorrows (*gham*), and dancing is equivalent to *surur* (cheerfulness, exhilaration), which is a valid movement or activity.[6] Among the recommended norms in *adab-i-sama* is included the suggestion that if a fellow participant stands up in *wajd*, moved or transported in an ecstasy of love for God, then others in the *majlis* should follow him in standing up to be by his side. And, while dancing in ecstasy (*raqs*), he should maintain a certain degree of grace so that others are not put off by his vulgar movements and intention.[7] Though it takes two to tango, the dance companion's role should be to help him in reaching out for the God above.

Nizamuddin Auliya is also quoted as saying that the body movement that is generated in remembering God in ecstasy is *mustahab*, a recommended or allowed practice, and if the intention is for some carnal pleasure (*fasad*), then it is *haram*.[8] However, if a person gets really ecstatic (*raqs* and *harkat*) in *sama* and even tears his clothes, he may be treated as one overpowered by ecstasy and so he may not be questioned. But those who pretend to be lost in ecstasy just to show off their spiritual bent of mind will be accused of indulging in *haram*.[9] Sufi circles did identify the pretenders who would be the cause of embarrassment, especially when the *ulama* were ready to interrogate anyone departing from norms of proper conduct. *Qalandars* and related groups particularly attracted attention for their behaviour, which could be identified as deviance. Also, Nizamuddin's followers themselves would be reported for being part of musical jamborees where not only instruments were used, but also women were present – much to the disappointment of the khwaja. However, it might appear that Nizamuddin maintained some ambiguity in the matter, or at least let the followers decide for themselves what was good for them, recalling here reports of his dearest disciple, Amir Khusrau, inventing not only *ragas, khayal* and *tarana,* but also being instrumental in creating the sitar, sarod, etc.

Amir Khwurd had noted that certain jurists and *ulama* who were opposed to *sama* would also come to observe the *majlis* organized by Nizamuddin Auliya. Observing the manner in which the shaikh would be standing at one place, crying silently and wiping his tears, even as the singers – two of whom are named as Hasan Paihadi and Samat Qawwal – were reciting heart-rending Persian poetry in their distinctive intonations, the *ulama* would fall at his feet and accept as legitimate what they would otherwise condemn as un-Islamic.[10] Despite being deeply touched by the poetry of love being recited by the singers and all but lost in the thought of the divine, Nizamuddin would not only come out of the hall, taking a break at the time of prayers, but also keep a watch on the activities of the other participants. He once noticed Amir Khusrau raising his hands during *raqs* as a Sufi would do and asked him not to do so as that would indicate he was attached to worldly concerns. Thereafter, Khusrau would dance with his hands down and palms closed, appearing as if his hands were tied and, unlike the Sufi, unable to break free and attempt to reach out for God.[11]

Hazrat Nizamuddin's interest in music and particular verses, which touched his soul and created ecstasy in him, would become very popular in the large circle of his followers. Some very good singers attached themselves to the khwaja. They would spend a lot of time training themselves, composing new *ghazals,* creating new *ragas* and taking the art to newer heights.[12] According to reports, not only sophisticated Persian poetry of love, but also Hindi verses would create ecstasy for Nizamuddin. On one occasion, the shaikh was overwhelmed by ecstasy (*haal*) for a long period after listening to some Hindi poetry composed by one of his Chishti successors (*khalifas*), Maulana Wajihuddin Yusuf.[13]

Eventually, Amir Khwurd wrote, the *naib hakim* (deputy governor) of the Sultanate under Ghiyasuddin Tughluq, Qazi Jalaluddin Lawanji, who was opposed to the lovers of God (*ahl-i-ishq*), that is, the Sufis, encouraged Shaikhzada Husamuddin, a disgruntled disciple of Nizamuddin Auliya who had access to the sultan's court, to build a case against the shaikh. It was reported to the sultan that Nizamuddin, who was a leading religious personality of the time, indulged in music that was considered *haram* in the *mazhab* of Imam Abu Hanifa, founder of the Hanafi school of jurisprudence, which the Sultanate *ulama* followed in their practise of Islam. The sultan was told that because of following Nizamuddin, thousands of others were fascinated by the unlawful practice of music. Amir Khwurd stated that Sultan Ghiyasuddin had no idea of the legality of music and, therefore, wondered how it was that a leading religious authority could indulge in an un-Islamic (*ghayr mashru*) act.[14]

To convince Sultan Ghiyasuddin, Hazrat Nizamuddin's opponents collected the works relating to music in the *shari'at,* which were used to issue *fatwas* against Hamiduddin Nagauri, another Sufi who famously loved music, and presented them to the ruler. The sultan was already uncomfortable with Nizamuddin's attitude, especially over the dispute regarding the recovery of cash-grants doled out by the usurper Khusrau Khan, who had killed the last Khalji sultan, Qutbuddin Mubarak Shah. He announced that if the religious scholars have issued *fatwas* against the legality of *sama,* then the Sufi shaikh should be brought to his presence, and the leading *ulama* of the city should also be summoned so that the problem can be discussed or debated in an assembly of the learned and the truth of the matter established. Hazrat Nizamuddin's followers who were employed in the sultan's court informed the shaikh, who apparently did not show any concern over the development. However, a number of other leading religious scholars of the time who had joined the discipleship of Nizamuddin Auliya, such as Maulana Fakhruddin Zarradi and Maulana Wajihuddin Pa'ili, began to scan the relevant texts to collect arguments in favour of the validity of the practice of *sama*.[15]

When Hazrat Nizamuddin eventually appeared in the court on the appointed date, he was accompanied by Maulana Fakhruddin, who was superior in reputation to the *naib hakim*, Qazi Jalaluddin, and Maulana Muhiuddin Kashani, another leading scholar of the age. As the arguments began, Qazi Jalaluddin lectured Nizamuddin on the need to mend his ways and warned him of being punished if he continued to organize music assemblies. Amir Khwurd noted that Nizamuddin listened silently to all the accusations levelled in harsh language, but Jalaluddin's warning of punishment provoked the shaikh to curse the opponent, first that he would lose his position as the *naib hakim* and would die soon after. Whatever may be the rational, historical account, Jalaluddin actually lost his position and died not long after the inquest.[16]

As the debate proceeded in front of the leading *ulama* of the city and a full house of nobles, Shaikhzada Husamuddin, Nizamuddin's former disciple, took over from the silenced Qazi Jalaluddin and asked the shaikh whether he would organize *sama* in his assemblies in which the participants danced, cried or raised slogans. Nizamuddin advised Husamuddin to refrain from showing his overenthusiasm, and instead of making unnecessary statements, explain what he meant by *sama.* Hazrat Nizamuddin's question on the need to first clarify the meaning of the term *sama* itself would test any theoretical grounding of the opponents in the terms and categories being deployed by them. Instead of explaining his understanding of the validity or otherwise of music, Husamuddin continued in a rhetorical mode and said that he did not know the meaning of *sama,* but so many great *ulama* have said that it was *haram.* Nizamuddin replied that if Husamuddin did not know the meaning of *sama,* he was not fit to discuss the matter. Thus, the main opponent in the case was also silenced.[17]

Amir Khwurd recorded that Ghiyasuddin Tughluq was carefully following the debate, and was asking the noisy opponents to keep quiet and listen to what the shaikh was saying. Of all the *ulama* present there, Maulana Hamiduddin and Maulana Shahabuddin Multani remained silent; they did not say anything scandalous from the point of view of the Sufi facing the inquest. According to Amir Khwurd, Hamiduddin did in fact intervene to say that the reports of the opponents regarding the details of the activities in Nizamuddin's *majlis* were not true, and that he had himself closely observed the participants, including shaikhs and dervishes. However, during the course of the discussion, another official *alim*, Qazi Kamaluddin, interjected to say that he had seen a report quoting Imam Abu Hanifa that *sama* was *haram* and *raqs* was *fasq* (sinful). Nizamuddin replied that there was no prohibition in the matter.[18]

As the arguments and counterarguments continued, Maulana Ilmuddin, a grandson of Bahauddin Zakaria (the thirteenth-century Suhrawardi saint of Multan), arrived at the court. The sultan turned towards Ilmuddin and, referring to him as a scholar and traveller, inquired whether *sama* was *halal* or *haram*. Ilmuddin replied that he had written a tract on the issue wherein he had collected all the arguments for and against music. His conclusion was that *sama* was permissible (*mubah*) for those who take it as a matter of the heart, and it was unlawful (*haram*) for those who indulge in it to satisfy their *nafs*, the lower self. The sultan further asked Ilmuddin whether, during his travels to Baghdad, Damascus and Rum, he had seen the Sufis of those cities listening to music, and whether anyone had stopped them from doing so. Ilmuddin said that the Sufis of those cities did listen to music, which was sometimes also accompanied by instruments like *daf* and *shababa*, but no one prevented them from following this practice, which was inherited from the time of the earliest masters, Shaikh Junaid and Shibli. The sultan was silenced on hearing this response from Ilmuddin, but the *naib hakim* spoke again, insisting that the sultan must announce a ban on music, keeping in mind Imam Abu Hanifa's opinion in the matter. However, the sultan eventually followed Shaikh Nizamuddin's request not to issue any order in this regard, and thus concluded, for Nizamuddin, on a happy note, the acrimonious debate in the *darbar*, which lasted for roughly the whole of the first half of the day, from *chasht* to *zuhar* prayers.[19]

Amir Khwurd's above narrative on the sultan being favourably disposed towards Nizamuddin and his acceptance of the shaikh's suggestion not to issue an order is derived from a reliable report of Fakhruddin Zarradi, who was present at the inquest and recorded the details in a text of his own. Amir Khwurd further noted that according to another less reliable report, the sultan had ordered that Nizamuddin could continue with his practice of *sama* and no one should prevent him from doing so. But others, like the *qalandars* and *haidaris*, who were suspected of listening to music for fun, should be prevented from doing so.[20] According to another report, unlike Imam Abu Hanifa, who is believed to have disapproved of *sama* as a whole, Imam Shafi'i, founder of the Shafi'i school of Sunni jurisprudence, not only considered *sama* a legitimate devotional practice, but also approved the use of musical instruments.[21]

Referring to the report in *Hasrat-nama* of Ziyauddin Barani, another important contemporary figure who, like Amir Khusrau, doubled up as a courtier as well as disciple of Nizamuddin Auliya, Amir Khwurd further wrote that after returning from the sultan's court at the time of the *zuhar* (afternoon) prayers, Nizamuddin called Maulana Muhiuddin Kashani and Amir Khusrau and told them of the disgusting behaviour of the *ulama* – not only of their personal opposition to him, but also of their disrespecting prophetic traditions (*hadis*) by privileging a report by a jurist, Imam Abu Hanifa. All the *hadis* referred to by Nizamuddin justifying the validity of his interest in Sufi music were dismissed as important only for Imam Shafi'i, and the Shafi'i school of jurisprudence was characterized as opposed to the Hanafi *mazhab* followed by the official *ulama* in Delhi. Expressing his concern that the *ulama's* approach could mislead the people into not having enough respect for the prophetic traditions, Nizamuddin prophesied that there would be a divine retribution for the wrong faith of the *ulama* of the city.[22]

Amir Khwurd concluded that within a period of four years, all the *ulama* of the opposing group were forced to migrate to Deogiri (renamed Daulatabad), most of them dying there. This is with reference to an order of the next sultan, Muhammad bin Tughluq, who had considerable respect for Hazrat Nizamuddin. The city itself was faced with famine and epidemic. The shaikh's prophecy proved true, and the legitimacy of his practice was not only approved by the sultan, but also confirmed through divine intervention.[23] Indeed, Sultan Ghiyasuddin himself died under mysterious circumstances in a camp outside Delhi; this, once again, happened at a time when he was ordering the shaikh to leave the city, provoking the latter to utter that proverbial phrase, *hunuz dilli dur ast* (Delhi is yet far away for you)!

Irrespective of the exact historicity of the incident and whether those developments were related to Nizamuddin's curse or political connections, what cannot be denied is that the shaikh was considerably irritated by the opposition to his mystical practices. In *Fawa'id-ul-Fu'ad*, which was being compiled by Amir Hasan Sijzi during the period that coincided with the debate in Ghiyasuddin's court, the shaikh is found explaining his position in self-restrained agitation (neither cursing nor abusing the antagonists but deploying the language of the jurists). It is recorded that one of the members of the audience mentioned that the ruler had given orders to the effect that the shaikh could listen to music whenever he liked, and that it was lawful (*halal*) for him. Nizamuddin replied that what was *halal* could not become *haram* and vice versa just because someone had issued orders to this effect. However, the shaikh added, in a case like the current controversy over *sama* and the ruler's order, since Imam Shafi'i had termed *sama* as *mubah* (permissible) even when accompanied by instruments like *daf and chaghana*, which were not in conformity with the majority Hanafi position, it was the ruler's discretion to follow whichever position he found appropriate in his opinion.[24] Sultan Ghiyasuddin clearly followed the Shafi'i position in the matter, allowing the shaikh to continue with his practice, despite the uncomfortable relationship between the Sufi and the sultan.

Yet, in continuing to defend the legitimacy of music, Nizamuddin insisted that musical instruments such as *chang* and *rabab* should be completely avoided. When it was reported that some dervishes were found dancing (*raqs*) in a musical programme in which instruments were used, Nizamuddin maintained that it was not the right thing to do. He was informed that when confronted, the dervishes explained that they were so lost (in remembering God) that they had no idea musical instruments were being played there. According to Nizamuddin, this justification was not valid and could be used for covering any *gunah* or sin.[25]

Further, referring to the differences of opinion within Sufi fraternities on the validity of music as a legitimate spiritual exercise, Amir Hasan had mentioned that he had participated in the ongoing discussion at Nizamuddin's *jama'at-khana*. He had opined that while one could understand the *ulama's* opposition to *sama,* how should one explain the opposition of certain Sufis to the practice? He had also remarked that even if some Sufis considered *sama* as *haram*, they could avoid it instead of fighting with fellow Sufis, which was not the way of the dervishes. According to Amir Hasan, Hazrat Nizamuddin liked these observations and stated that there were so many *ulama* who did not say anything and yet an ignorant fellow (*na-waqif*) was fighting (the shaikh was clearly referring to the disgruntled disciple who had lost the case in the sultan's court).[26]

Amir Hasan further noted that the shaikh also liked his remark that the opponents of *sama* were known to him and that they would not have taken any interest in music even if there were no two opinions on its lawfulness. Nizamuddin opined that such people actually lacked the *zauq* or taste for music and had no basis or orientation for its appreciation.[27] The pleasure of music is appreciated better by someone who is filled with pain (*dard)* for the divine beloved and endures it gracefully. In exceptional cases, an outward expression of madness, as in Majnun's love for Laila, is also recommended.

The reports of Nizamuddin Auliya's struggle to defend Sufi music and the elimination of the key opponents in quick succession became a part of Sufi memory. While recounting the proceedings of the *mahzar* from the *Siyar-ul-Auliya,* Shaikh Jamali had provided the background of the conflict in his early sixteenth-century text, *Siyar-ul-Arifin*. He wrote that after the brutal murder of Qutbuddin Mubarak Shah, his usurping successor, Khusrau Khan, had distributed large sums to the dervishes in the city. Three Sufis of note had refused to accept these offerings, but Nizamuddin Auliya took the 5,00,000 *tankas*, which had been sent to him, and distributed them amongst the poor. Others who had received the grants kept them in trust. Four months later, when Ghiyasuddin Tughluq defeated Khusrau Khan and ascended the throne, he sought to recover the funds, which had left the treasury depleted. Nizamuddin Auliya argued that the money he had received was from the public treasury. He had, therefore, given it to the deserving, spending nothing on himself. The sultan was silenced by this reply, but his heart turned against the shaikh. The controversy over the legality of *sama* came in handy for the king to call a *mahzar.* The proceedings came to an end with the ruler expressing his regret for summoning the saint to the court. No sooner had the shaikh returned to his hospice than news arrived that the sovereign was very ashamed and had dismissed Qazi Jalaluddin from his post.[28]

Through this inquest, Hazrat Nizamuddin was

forced to break the Chishti principle of not visiting the sultan's court. He was compelled to appear at the monarch's court and submit to judgement. This had serious repercussions as the *naib hakim*, who was instrumental in calling the *mahzar*, was removed from the post. The *ulama* who had opposed the saint were forcibly sent off to Daulatabad. Famine and epidemic haunted the capital city, *dar-ul-khilafat*, for decades. The sultan himself did not last for long. His death at the outskirts of the capital shortly after the event and bestowal of kingship upon prince Juna Khan (Muhammad Tughluq) by Nizamuddin Auliya is mentioned in the *Qiwam-ul-Aqa'id*, an early biography – anecdotal and hagiographic – but they are not linked to the above encounter.[29] However, as mentioned above, all the opponents were soon eliminated, dying unnatural death – believed in Sufi memory as the result of Hazrat Nizamuddin's curse. Provoking the wrath of accomplished Sufi saints could be a flawed strategy.

The Sufis emphasized on uniting the people into an emotional, devotional or spiritual community, creating conditions for respectful coexistence of all the diversity the society is known for. Thus, uniting people and not dividing them has been the cardinal mantra. On their part, the *qawwals* have continued to sing the songs of love for God and devotion for the Prophet. As a leading Sufi poet rhetorically put it: only a donkey has no sense of music; and some others counterpoised that even the donkey loved music.[30] Only some heartless men could oppose it, legally or otherwise. In either case, it was a scandal that was resolved in favour of friends and lovers of God, led by the leading Chishti saint of Delhi, Hazrat Nizamuddin Auliya. Disappointed over the unsavoury episode, Nizamuddin could tell the opponents:

Gufti ke beh nazad-i man haram-ast sama
Gar bar tu haram-ast haramat bada

You say that *sama* was *haram* for you
If it is *haram* for you let it remain *haram*.[31]

10

RECITATION OF PERSIAN POETRY

U sukhan az kushtan-i man mi-kunad
Man be-hamin khush keh sukhan mi-kunad

He speaks about killing me
I am glad at least he speaks about me.

– Hazrat Nizamuddin Auilya,
as quoted in *Fawa'id-ul-Fu'ad*

The above couplet recited by Hazrat Nizamuddin Auliya refers to the powers of patience and endurance in the mystic path and tiring out the wicked antagonists.[1] Indeed, devotional movements invoke powerful and emotionally charged poetry both for ecstasy and as protest or resistance against the entrenched custodians of the moral code of conduct imposed by opponents. Hazrat Nizamuddin recited and heard exquisite Persian poetry while speaking to his followers or listening to *qawwali*. The content of the fine poetical compositions which were recited or sung in *qawwali* performances once again reveal that the opposition from sections of the *ulama* was completely uncalled for, even from within the standpoint of what was recommended in Islam and what was forbidden. Hazrat Nizamuddin recited and heard verses composed by some of the great Iranian Persian poets, such as Khaqani, Nizami, Hafiz, Sa'di and other near-contemporary stalwarts, who were setting high standards of excellence in the thirteenth and early fourteenth centuries. Nizamuddin would also quote his Chishti predecessors for verses they recited of their own and of others. He would also frequently switch to poetry and recite verses he had himself composed. Some fine poets grew around him as well. These include Amir Khusrau and Amir Hasan Sijzi, besides a number of other lesser-known poets. Some samples of Persian poetry have been provided in the previous pages to bolster some of the arguments through those powerful expressions in verses. In this chapter, some more examples from the large corpus of Persian poetry will be presented to illustrate the value of the contents of these compositions on the Sufi idea of love (*ishq*), love for God, ethical precepts, kindness and mercy, etc.

Poetry of Love and Sufi Ecstasy

For Hazrat Nizamuddin, there was a contradiction between love (*ishq*) and intellect (*aql*). The *ulama* were people of intellect (*ahl-i-aql*) and the Sufi dervishes were people of love (*ahl-i-ishq*). The intellect of scholars overpowers love, and the mystics' love dominates intellect. According to him, the person of the prophets, showcasing higher credentials, encapsulates both the characteristics of love and intellect. The powerful emotions of love can go beyond control and those who cannot stand it should shut their ears as well, for poetry catering to overwhelming desires is not easily understood by people devoid of feelings of love:

> *Aql ra ba-ishq gush nist zoodash panbeh kun*
>
> There's no hearing for love before intellect, stuff
> it with cotton soon![2]

Some Sufis went further to observe that expressions of love were above regular piety and prayers. Ali

Khokhari of Multan would declare that he would not have anything to do with a person devoid of feelings of love and pain. He would comment that such a person was nothing; he had no sense of love. Nizamuddin observed that Ali Khokhari would incorrectly pronounce *ishq* as *ishak*, as in the local vernacular, but knew what he meant! He further remarked that an early Sufi master in Central Asia, Yahiya Ma'az Raazi, had preached that even a small component of love was superior to all the prayers and devotions of humans and fairies counted together (*yak zarreh muhabbat beh az ta'ate jumle aadmiyan o pariyaan*). Related to the theme of love was the observation, by Hazrat Nizamuddin, that his preceptor, Shaikh Fariduddin, used to bless people by remarking that God may give you pain, which was understood as blessings for kindness and love, which meant enduring pain.[3]

Sometimes, one Persian couplet was enough to send a Sufi deep into an exhilarating bliss (*surur*). Hazrat Nizamuddin mentioned during a conversation on metaphors and allegories in poetry, especially verses on love (*ghazal*), how Shaikh Fariduddin repeatedly recited a particular couplet for several hours during the day, and kept repeating it at dusk and all night all the way to the morning:

Nizami in cheh israr ast ke-az khaatir ayaan kar di
Kasi sarash nami daanad zabaan dar kash zabaan dar kash

Nizami, what are these secrets you have revealed from the depth inside
No will understand these here, keep your mouth shut.

Nizamuddin said no one knew the thoughts that were making Shaikh Fariduddin recite the couplet again and again. Every time, he would look perplexed and go into ecstasy (*har baar keh mi-guft taghaiyiri dar wi paida mi-aayad*).[4]

Speaking in the same *majlis*, Hazrat Nizamuddin also informed the audience how once the eminent Suhrawardi saint of Multan, Shaikh Bahauddin Zakaria, was standing at the door inside his house, holding the two panels with each hand, and repeatedly reciting this couplet:

Kardi sanama bar sar-i ma baar-i digar
Ma hich na-kardim khuda mi-daanad

My love, you have put another burden on my head
I have done nothing, God is witness.[5]

Nizamuddin added that the feeling of spiritual bliss remained the personal experience of Shaikh Bahauddin – a private matter expressed through poetry. In any case, personal spiritual experiences of the Sufis were to be kept secret and not shared with the public. The execution of Mansur al-Hallaj in 922 CE in Baghdad, for going public with his experience of feeling the presence of God inside his person, making him utter 'I am the truth' or 'I am God (*anal haq*)' was a continuous reminder that spiritual experiences were private matters of the mystics. Ecstasy caused in the course of meditation or caused by reciting the Qur'an, chanting *zikr* formulae or listening to poetry can be visibly expressed, but should not be uttered. Hold your tongue, as the verses above reminded Shaikh Fariduddin.

Examples of poetry composed in praise of Shaikh Fariduddin and presented to him could also be touching and cause ecstasy, as in this example of a quatrain sent by a mystic friend Qazi Hamiduddin Nagauri, as part of a letter written to him (Shaikh Fariduddin):

Aan aql kuja keh dar kamaal-i tu rasad
Wa aan ruh kuja keh dar jalaal-i tu rasad
Giram keh tu pardeh bar girafti ze jamaal

Aan dideh kuja keh dar jamaal tu rasad

Where is that wisdom which could reach your perfection
And, where is the soul which could reach your grandeur
Agreed, you have removed the veil from your graceful presence
But where is the eye which could behold your beauty.[6]

Shaikh Fariduddin was overpowered with the desire to listen to poetry (*sama*), but no *qawwal* was around, so the letter with the above quatrain was read out by his close companion and servant, Badruddin Ishaq. According to Hazrat Nizamuddin, just a few opening lines from the letter sent Shaikh Fariduddin into deep ecstasy (*yak haali wa zauqi paida shud*). Nizamuddin mentioned another letter written by Shaikh Badruddin Ghaznavi, a fellow disciple of Khwaja Qutbuddin Bakhtiyar Kaki, to Shaikh Fariduddin, which included these two couplets:

Farid-i din o millat yaar-i mihtar
Keh baadash dar karamat zindagani
Diregha khatiram gar jame' boodi
Be-madhash kard mi shakar feshani

Farid, the superior friend of the faith and
community
May his life be blessed with miracles
Alas! If I had a composed mind
I would sing sweet songs in his praise.[7]

Like most early Chishti masters, Shaikh Badruddin Ghaznavi was also deeply affected by poetry recitation in *mahfil-i-sama*. According to Hazrat Nizamuddin, even when Badruddin Ghaznavi had become old and was not even able to properly stand and walk, he would get into ecstasy while listening to *ghazals* recited by the *qawwals* and start dancing. When some people would comment on how the old man was able to dance, he would reply that the old man does not dance, it is the love which dances; wherever there is love, there is dance as well.[8]

The most touching example of poetry of love causing tremendous upheaval inside the heart and mind of a Sufi is that of Shaikh Fariduddin's preceptor, Khwaja Qutbuddin Bakhtiyar Kaki. The latter died listening to the same couplet for several days, following its recitation in a *mahfil-i-sama*:

Kushtagaan-i khanjar-i taslim ra
Har zaman az ghayb jani-ye digar-ast

The victims of the dagger of submission
Get a new life from the unseen every moment.[9]

A music aficionado going into ecstasy after listening to a particular couplet sung by a *qawwal* and passing away listening to it for several days became something of a Sufi folklore. Further, according to Hazrat Nizamuddin, Bakhtiyar Kaki frequently recited this quatrain (*rubayi*):

Sauda-ye tu andar dil-i diwana-i maast
Har ja keh hadis toost afsana-i maast
Biganeh keh az tu guft aan khwish man-ast
Khwishi keh na az tu guft begana-i maast

Your love resides inside my intoxicated heart
Wherever you are discussed my story also exists
Stranger who speaks of you belongs to me
Relative who doesn't speak of you becomes a stranger.[10]

There is nothing un-Islamic in the examples of Sufi poetry presented above. Custodians of Islam of different kinds are habituated to hurl *fatwas* against one another on what is recommended in Islam and what is forbidden. In the process, they belittle and even harm each other. The Sufis' fascination with the love of God has similarly been seen in sceptical terms by naysayers of all hues. Medieval Sufis themselves were confident of breaking all boundaries between humans and God and between human beings themselves. Hazrat Nizamuddin Auliya emphasized the need to transcend juridical boundaries in matters such as the permissibility of Sufi music and the legitimacy of the Sufi idea of love. When Amir Hasan Sijzi, compiler of *Fawa'id-ul-Fu'ad*, reminded him through a line of a verse that Imam Abu Hanifa, the founder of the Hanafi school of Sunni jurisprudence, had nothing to say on love, Hazrat Nizamuddin added that Imam Shafi'i didn't say anything on it either. Thus, the Sufi idea of love is beyond the restricted boundaries of the four schools of Sunni jurisprudence called *mazaahib*. It is a personal matter – a matter of the heart – between human beings and the all-knowing Creator.

Sufi traditions have continuously emphasized the need for patience and forbearance even under extreme provocation. Collections of conversations of medieval Sufis are full of poetic compositions recommending grace and kindness to even the most inveterate of opponents and enemies. Anger, aggression and bigotry are to be completely shunted out from one's personal conduct. Instead, prayers for mercy, peace and well-being are the recommended response. Aggressive feelings of revenge should give way to regards and blessings. Emphasizing these virtues which need to be cultivated, Hazrat Nizamuddin Auliya frequently quoted some fine Persian couplets which sum up everything said above. He reiterated that if revenge is the order of the day, there will be violence and unrest all around. He also pointed out that it was easy to be nice to people who are kind; the challenge and recommendation was to be nice to bad people as well. Even while complaining and arguing, it should be done in the politest manner, speaking softly and avoiding cursing and shouting. Certainly not in a manner where a person's neck's veins get swollen shouting in rage. In sum, behave like decent human beings, not like beastly creatures. Cultivate love and peace in one's heart, rather than hatred and violence.

Desire for Union and Pangs of Separation

A heart devoted to love for God and by implication for all his creations will necessarily suffer from desire for love and deal with pangs of separation. Physical desire was certainly done away with the pleasures of the heart, which could be cultivated through fine conversations, powerfully expressed poetry of love and sense of peace accrued from the recitation of the Qur'an. Sometimes, beautifully composed letters sent by fellow Sufis could touch the heart. Effects of good company and time spent together with kind friends devoted to the mystic path and emotions thus generated could be expressed through excellent poetical compositions.

Amir Hasan Sijzi has recorded in *Fawa'id-ul-Fua'd* that once he came to meet Hazrat Nizamuddin Auliya after a gap of eight months. Some others from the army, fellow officers and disciples, were also visiting Hazrat Nizamuddin that day. There was a lot of discussion about overpowering feeling of love and affection (*ishtiyaq*) and that the Sufi master was deeply missed because of their inability to meet him (*firaaq*). During the conversation, Hazrat Nizamuddin mentioned how he once wrote a letter to his preceptor, Shaikh Fariduddin. He added this quatrain (*rubayi*) in that letter:[11]

Ze aan ruyi keh bandeh-i tu khwanand ma ra
Bar mardumak-i dideh nishanand ma ra
Lutf-i aamat inayati farmudeh ast
Warna cheh kasam cheh danand ma ra

People love me,
Because I am known to be a slave of yours.
Your love for all has blessed me with a kind favour,
Otherwise, what I am that people should know me.[12]

Amir Hasan has also recorded that once he came to meet some relatives in the vicinity of the hospice of Hazrat Nizamuddin and thought that he should drop in to see him as well. In the Chishti fraternity, it was believed that unplanned visits should be avoided. But Amir Hasan told himself that even if the custom was such, he would not leave without seeing Nizamuddin. So, he broke the custom and went away to meet the master. Appreciating the overwhelming desire of the disciple, Hazrat Nizamuddin assured him that he did the right thing by coming over. Suited to the occasion, Nizamuddin also recited this couplet defying established norms of proper conduct:

Dar kuyi kharabaat wa sarai aubaash
Man'a nabud biya wa benashin wa bebaash

In the lanes of taverns and dwellings of the
ruffians
There are no restrictions; come, sit and stay.[13]

Hazrat Nizamuddin further observed that the general practice with the Sufi masters was that people would not visit them before *Chaasht* (early morning) and after *'Asr* (late afternoon) prayers, which meant meeting during the day. But this was not the case in his hospice; anyone could drop in at any time.[14]

Amir Hasan wrote, that the same day, the conversation between Hazrat Nizamuddin and his followers moved to topics such as people returning from *hajj* and remaining unreconstructed in terms of proper conduct, the idea of service (*khidmat*) and submission to the will of God (*raza*) and manners relating to grace and dignity. With regard to the question of grace and beauty (*husn*), Hazrat Nizamuddin remarked that someone had versified ten recommended practices (*sunna* or traditions relating to Prophet Muhammad), five of which were concerned with the head and the remaining five with the body. Not impressed with mere versification without adopting the message in one's life, Nizamuddin countered with a verse of his own:

Dah sukhan dar do bait aawardi
Kaar kun kaar ke-in hame sukhan-ast

You have covered ten topics in two couplets
Act, put into practice, else it is just talk.[15]

Action following the path of the Prophet as part of his community (*ahl-i sunnat wal jama'at*) is continuously stressed in the Sufi fraternity and, thus, in the conversations of Hazrat Nizamuddin Auliya as well. We shall turn to the frequent refrain for guidance from the traditions and practices of the Prophet in the next chapter. It will be appropriate to conclude this chapter with Hazrat Nizamuddin Auliya's observation that fine pieces of poetry were acceptable in Islam, as per a tradition of the Messenger of God (Prophet Muhammad), who has said that certainly some poetical compositions are words of wisdom (*inna mina-ash-she'r le-hikmah*). So, the distinction was between heart-touching verses recited in a fine voice and vulgar compositions which do not appeal to a kind heart. Nizamuddin went on to remark, with reference to the validity of the usual exaggeration by the poets, that he had seen in a famous book that uttering falsehood was a sinful act, but incorrect statements in poetry were not a matter of sin (*dar kitabi mashhur dideh ast keh kazb ra asmi ast amma kazbi keh dar she'r guyand dar aan asmi nist*). In general, old age and the teachings of Islam were considered sufficient to keep a person away from sins (*kaf-ash-shaybo wal-islamo lilmar-e naahiyan*).[16] In all cases, Islamic intellectual traditions have always privileged recitation of Qur'anic verses over poetical compositions of the poets, even when the latter were expressing matters of pain and sorrow in their work. The need for continuous guarding of the lower self and for remaining within the fold of *shari'at*, even while following the mystic path (*tariqat*), shows that the Sufis were conscious of adhering to the practices of the Prophet, and thus used his ways to accomplish their desire to reach the beloved God and the reality of his presence (*haqiqat*). Powerful mystical poetry had the ability to transport the accomplished connoisseur to that ultimate reality. Overpowered by emotions, Sufis could chant:

> *Az bahr-i tu miram ze baray tu zeem*
>
> We live for Him and die for Him.[17]

11

FOLLOWING THE PATH OF THE PROPHET

Allahumma aj-alni mahsudan wa la taj-alni haasidan

O God, make me an object of envy and do not make me envious of others.

– Tradition of the Prophet (*hadis*), quoted by Hazrat Nizamuddin Auliya

Hazrat Nizamuddin Auliya's life and teachings were marked by a strict adherence to what was recommended in the Qur'an and the traditions of Prophet Muhammad. Hazrat Nizamuddin and his Chishti predecessors were especially committed to being part of the blessed community of the followers of the Prophet (*ahl-i sunnat wal jama'at*). For all the mystical experiences in the Sufi *tariqat*, often not understandable to ordinary human beings, the Chishti practitioners insisted on remaining within the bounds of *shari'at*. Nizamuddin's conversations with his disciples were, therefore, continuously marked by insights and guidance from the Qur'an and *sunnat* (practices) of the Prophet. This was not only so as individuals, as in the quotation given above, but also as part of the community (congregation, *jama'at* or *umma*). The insistence on love and devotion for the Prophet and following him strictly as a role model and being part of the exalted community of his followers will be discussed in this chapter.

Continuous self-appraisal in terms of a human being's relations with God and with other human beings and following the path shown by the Prophet of Islam is critical to the practices of the Sufis. In the *hadis* quoted above, the refrain highlights the excellence of the ethical self that could serve as the object of someone's envy, rather than someone envious of others. Hazrat Nizamuddin explained that there were two kinds of feelings here: *hasad* (envy or jealousy) and *ghabta* (desirous to be like another, that is, ungrudging emulation of someone's excellence). The negative envious emotion (*hasad*) induces one to wish the ruin of a person who is happy and prospering. The positive emotion of appreciation of the goodness and excellence of others (*ghabta*) makes a person feel good and aspire for similar blessings in one's life. Thus, *hasad* is *haram* or forbidden and *ghabta* is legitimate.[1]

The complete trust (*tawakkul*) in God, as recommended by the Prophet, meant all aspects of one's life were taken care of, including temporary adversities. These were viewed as part of the creator's wisdom, including such matters as means of sustenance (*rizq*). The Supreme Being has assured basic creature comforts for everyone, besides other surprising bounties previously assured or not. Depending on what was on offer from the divine treasury, there were four kinds of sustenance: *rizq-i-mazmun*, *rizq-i-maqsum*, *rizq-i-mamluk* and *rizq-i-mau'ud*. Hazrat Nizamuddin's insightful explanation of these bounties of God will be appropriate to mention here. The first variety (*rizq-i-mazmun*) is what one gets in the form of food and drink, which is sufficient for one's sustenance. It means the Almighty has taken it upon himself to provide, as in this Qura'nic verse (Surah Hood, Verse 6): *wa ma min daa-bbatin fil arze illa al-allahe rizqoha* (there is no moving creature on earth whose sustenance doesn't depend on Allah). Full trust in God takes care of the basic requirements of life. The second category (*rizq-i-maqsum*) has been earmarked from eternity and is recorded on the preserved tablet (*lauh-i-mahfuz*), that is, it is written in their fate; the third kind (*rizq-i-mamluk*) is one's own savings, wealth, money, clothes and other valuables and the fourth (*rizq-i-mau'ud*) is the sustenance promised by God, especially for his righteous devotees. This is in accordance with the Qur'an (Surah Talaq, Verses 2–3: *wa man-yyataqi-llaha yaj-al lahu makhrajan-wa-yarzuqo min haiso la-yahtasibo* [and for him who fears Allah, he ever prepares a way out, and he provides for him from sources he had never imagined]).[2]

Hazrat Nizamuddin also reiterated the assumption that God particularly favoured the followers of Prophet Muhammad, who were given many concessions. The followers of previous prophets were advised to pray many times a day and only in dedicated places of worship (*masjid*). The followers of the Prophet Muhammad were advised to pray five times a day only and in a congregation, not only in a mosque but wherever possible. The emphasis on congregational prayers for a feeling of equality in brotherhood and community meant that even two persons could make a congregation (*jama'at*). Similarly, the ancient people were required to pay one-fourth of their wealth as religious tax (*zakat*); the followers of the Prophet were expected to pay only 5 dirams out of 200, that is, only 2.5 per cent of their accumulated wealth. Hazrat Nizamuddin explained that the person who paid 5 dirams out of 200 was not called a miser (*bakhil*), but people would not call him generous (*sakhi*) either. Generous was someone who gave something more than the prescribed percentage.[3]

Amir Hasan Sijzi, the accomplished compiler of Hazrat Nizamuddin's *malfuzat,* mentioned that he had asked Nizamuddin what he thought of a tradition of the Prophet, which said: *as-sakhiyyo habibu-llahe wa in kana faasiqan* (a generous person was a friend of God even if he was a sinner). Nizamuddin replied that people say so, wishing to remain ambiguous. Participating in the discussion, a disciple present in the *majlis* at the saint's hospice said that it was included in the collection of forty traditions (*Arba'yin*) of the Prophet. The shaikh commented that prophetic reports collected in the two authentic collections (*Sahi Muslim* and *Sahi Bukhari*) are correct (*aanche dar sahihain ast aan sahi ast*).[4] On several other occasions, there were discussions on the authenticity of particular prophetic reports, and Nizamuddin educated his disciples on the basis of his own education as a scholar of the traditions of the Prophet, which he had studied in Badaun and Delhi. Similar discussions on the accurate readings of the Qur'an and its reliable commentaries are also recorded in Hazrat Nizamuddin's teachings, in which the saint is seen guiding his disciples to follow practices which were considered correct in Sufi fraternities in the light of their long-standing investment in early sources of Islamic tradition.

Returning to the discussion on generosity and giving away one's wealth in alms and charity, Hazrat Nizamuddin observed that there was a distinction between generous (*sakhi*) and beneficent (*jawaad*). The generous person gave something more than the required minimum 2.5 per cent on one's wealth in *zakat*, whereas the beneficent person kept only 2.5 per cent, giving away the rest in charity. Nizamuddin also informed his disciples that his spiritual master, Shaikh Fariduddin, had identified three kinds of *zakat*: *zakat-i-shari'at*, *zakat-i-tariqat* and *zakat-i-haqiqat*. Giving 5 dirams out of 200 was *zakat-i-shari'at*; giving away all but 5 dirams was *zakat-i-tariqat* and *zakat-i-haqiqat* was giving away everything that one possessed, not keeping anything for oneself, which is the way of the Sufis.[5]

Hazrat Nizamuddin Auliya also informed his

followers that an excellent scholar of the traditions of the Prophet, Maulana Raziuddin Hasan Saghani (1181–1252), contributed significantly to the field, whose book, *Mashariq-ul-Anwar*, was a must-read in the Delhi Sultanate. It contained over 2,000 sayings of the Prophet, which were selected from the two most authoritative collections (*Sahi Muslim* and *Sahi Bukhari*). Hazrat Nizamuddin had himself studied *Mashariq-ul-Anwar* with a reputed scholar in Delhi. Maulana Saghani had written that his book was his credential before God (*hujjat*) and that if he ever faced any difficulty in ascertaining the authenticity of a *hadis*, he would see Prophet Muhammad in a dream and, following his advice, record the matter in its correct form. Like Hazrat Nizamuddin, Maulana Saghani was also from Badaun and later moved to Kaul (Aligarh) to serve as deputy to a local treasury officer (*mushrif*). The latter was an able but short-tempered person. One day, he said something at which Saghani smiled. Feeling offended, the officer threw the ink pot at him, which Saghani dodged. He then stood up and left the place, saying that he should not have associated himself with such illiterate characters (*jahhaal*). Following this incident, he returned to his studies and also offered tuition to the son of the magistrate (*haakim*) of Kaul. The small amount received was sufficient for his sustenance.[6]

Later, Maulana Raziuddin Saghani decided to go for *hajj* and also possibly to further his study of prophetic traditions. Many medieval Indian scholars of traditions of the Prophet (*muhaddis*) had travelled to Arabia for pursuing their higher studies. Some had stayed back and others returned. Maulana Saghani also spent time in Baghdad before relocating to Delhi. According to Nizamuddin Auliya, the Sultanate capital at that time had several top-class scholars of Islamic studies. Saghani was considered equal to them, but within the field of the study of traditions of the Prophet, he enjoyed a distinction which no one could surpass (*dar 'ilm-i hadis az hameh mumtaz bood wa heech kas muqabil-i u na-bood*).[7] A report in which he is said to have corrected a reputed teacher of *hadis* in Baghdad added to Saghani's credentials as one of the most reliable scholars of prophetic traditions, internationally. Hazrat Nizamuddin's recounting of the episode may be presented here to highlight the significance of the insistence on accuracy in dealing with traditions relating to Prophet Muhammad, which is of enduring significance for leading a properly guided Muslim life.

Ibn Zuhri, a renowned scholar of the life and

teachings of the Prophet, conducted regular classes in Baghdad, which were attended by many leading scholars of the city. He would sit on a specially built pulpit for his lectures, and scholars would sit in front of him in graded circles according to their learning; the more able ones would sit in the front, the lesser ones behind them and all others in the rows at the back. He would dictate the *hadis*, and scholars would write them down. One day, Maulana Raziuddin Saghani attended Ibn Zuhri's lecture, taking his seat in a circle quite at a distance from the front row. Ibn Zuhri was narrating a *hadis* on the subject of repeating the phrases of the calls for prayers (*azaan*) quietly, that is, the listener should repeat what the *mu'azzin* (the person who calls for prayers) had said. The eminent scholar had started narrating the *hadis* with the phrase *iza sakaba al-mu'azzin*, which suggested that as soon as one heard the words uttered by the *mu'azzin*, one should repeat what he had said. Maulana Saghani said in a low voice to the people sitting close to him that it was *iza sakata* – that is, when the *mu'azzin* had completed a particular phrase and paused – that people were required to repeat what he had said. Someone nearby passed it on to others, and eventually it reached the ears of Ibn Zuhri. He immediately asked who had said this.

Maulana Saghani said: 'I have said it.' Reflecting on the two expressions (*iza sakaba* and *iza sakata*), Ibn Zuhri announced that, as both seemed relevant, this should be checked in the book. After the lecture ended, they searched in the relevant books and found that both the phrases were recorded therein, but *iza sakata* was mentioned as more authentic. This news was brought to the notice of the caliph, who granted Maulana Saghani an audience. The caliph honoured him and performed the ritual of reading something before him, indicating that he accepted him as a teacher.[8]

Although such global recognition can make a scholar arrogant, this was not the case with Saghani. Hazrat Nizamuddin informed his followers that when Maulana Saghani returned to Delhi from his sojourn abroad with greater knowledge and distinction, Sanghani told his friends that there was a time when his teacher in Badaun, renowned for piety and saintliness, had refused to lend him his copy of a collection of *hadis*, *Mulakhhkhas*. Now, a hundred authors of such books come to be taught by him. There is no dearth of mischief makers around. Someone conveyed this remark of Maulana Saghani to his former teacher in Badaun. The veteran teacher observed: it appears that his *hajj* was not accepted well by God; had his *hajj* been accepted, he would not have spoken in that manner. On his part, Hazrat Nizamuddin remained respectful of Maulana Saghani's credentials as a sincere and pious scholar.[9] His book, *Mashariq-ul-Anwar*, remained an important source of guidance for him. Indeed, Hazrat Nizamuddin frequently referred to and taught from this book to his disciples.[10]

While dealing with excessive deference to the traditions of the Prophet to the extent that there were apprehensions about their authenticity, Hazrat Nizamuddin advised his disciples to refrain from passing judgement on whether a particular *hadis* was authentic or false. Instead, he suggested, caution and decorum required that they should say there was no record of it in such collections which have acquired reliability (*kitabi keh ahadis jama' kardeh-and wa i'tibaar yaafteh ni-aamdeh ast*).[11] Further, mastery over thousands of reports on the sayings and practices of the Prophet was no mean feat. The best preachers go prepared for the sermon and, while speaking extempore, refer to a few traditions and sometimes perhaps forget all the relevant ones. Hazrat Nizamuddin mentioned an interesting example of what transpired during a speech by Qazi Minhaj-us-Siraj Juzjani, the author of *Tabaqat-i-*

Nasiri, a celebrated history of Islam written in the middle of the thirteenth century and named after Sultan Nasiruddin Mahmud, son of the more celebrated early Delhi Sultan, Shamsuddin Iltutmish.

Hazrat Nizamuddin informed his audience that once Qazi Minhaj-us-Siraj was delivering a sermon and mentioned that as many as six related traditions had come together with uninterrupted chains of narrators. These included: one, speaking evil of an absent person is more outrageous than adultery (*al-ghibato ashaddo min-az-zina*); two, one who smelled a rose and did not recite *durud* for me was indeed cruel to me (*man shamma al-warda wa lam yosalla alayya faqad jafani*); three, the burden of proof lies with the plaintiff and oath is to be taken by the respondent who denies the accusation (*al-baynato ala-al-muddayi wal-yamino ala man ankar*). After repeating these three *hadis* of the Prophet, Hazrat Nizamuddin smiled and added that after reciting these three *hadis*, Qazi Minhaj-us-Siraj said that he did not know the remaining three; if someone scoffed at him for not knowing them, he would reply that the person scoffing at him had learned at least three *hadis*, which he previously did not know.[12]

Further, speaking about the virtues and excellence of *hadis* recitation and with reference to the three of them mentioned above, Hazrat Nizamuddin said that an eminent scholar, Maulana Raziuddin Nishapuri once fell ill and his health was deteriorating. A concerned scholar (*danishmand*) who lived in the vicinity of the maulana's house came to see him. Finding his condition critical, the scholar sat close to his pillow and recited the first of the three sayings of the Prophet: backbiting was more outrageous than adultery. Though suffering from the agony of his illness, the maulana asked the scholar what the context was for narrating this *hadis*, when there was no discussion about adultery or backbiting. The scholar replied that he was not bothered about the advisability of narrating the *hadis* at the moment, but he had heard that if an authentic prophetic report (*sahi hadis*) was narrated by the side of an ailing person, they would recover from the disease. He added that the *hadis* recited, wishing his recovery from illness and regaining his health was authentic and of an uninterrupted chain of narrators. Maulana Raziuddin did not say anything, but he gradually recovered from his illness.[13]

The Sufis believed in complete surrender to the will of God and enduring pain, as something sent by His majesty himself, as part of a wisdom that said to fall sick was somehow a good omen, a precursor to a larger good. Illnesses caused by some extra and unlawful sources, such as black magic and evil eye, were also to be taken as some divine expedience (*maslahat*). Sufis also believed that continually invoking the blessings of Prophet Muhammad would help in all cases of adversities, and even when there were none. Responsibly narrating the *hadis* was considered an act of piety that required extraordinary caution. Mentioning his recording of the utterances of Hazrat Nizamuddin Auliya, Amir Hasan Sijzi writes in the beginning of the fourth volume of *Fawa'id-ul-Fu'ad* that he had brought the first part of the compilation, as desired by the shaikh himself, for his kind perusal. Nizamuddin read it and obliged Sijzi with his generous approval and appreciation, commenting that he had written well, like a Sufi dervish, and its title, *Fawa'id-ul-Fua'd* (moral teachings benefiting the heart), was also commendable.[14]

Appropriate to the occasion, Amir Hasan further wrote about Hazrat Nizamuddin, telling the audience that Abu Hurairah had embraced Islam in the wake of the conquest of Khaibar, after which Prophet Muhammad lived for three years only. However, despite this short period of interaction, Abu Hurairah had narrated so many prophetic reports that they exceeded those narrated by all the companions of the Prophet taken together. For instance, the first caliph, Abu Bakr Siddiq, had narrated just three or four traditions of the Prophet and another close companion, Abdullah Ibn Abbas, less than ten. Another companion, Abdullah Ibn Mas'ud, who was a great jurist, narrated only one *hadis* during the whole span of his life. Abu Hurairah was asked how it was that he was able to commit such a large number of *hadis* to his memory and that too in such a short time, while others who had been in the company of the Prophet for a longer period were unable to do so. Abu Hurairah replied that the Prophet had assigned different duties to different companions, but he was retained in his own service. Thus, having the opportunity to be with him most of the time, he was able to memorize so many *hadis*. Hazrat Nizamuddin further related that once Abu Hurairah submitted to the Prophet that whatever he heard from him, he preserved in his memory, but he still missed some of his sayings. The Prophet said that if he wanted to remember what he heard from him, he should spread wide the skirt of his garment or a piece of cloth when the Prophet was speaking. Once he (the Prophet) had completed what he wanted to say, he (Abu Hurairah) should draw the cloth together slowly and bring his hand to his bosom.[15] This would ensure that Abu Hurairah would not forget anything the Prophet said.

Hazrat Nizamuddin then spoke about the companions of the Prophet, including four pious caliphs and three Abdullahs. This was followed by a reference to the virtues of Amirul Mu'minin Ali, in the course of which the khwaja quoted the Prophet as telling his companions: Ali was the best judge amongst them, as the most learned scholar will be the best of judges. Further, speaking about the mutual respect and consideration among the companions of the Prophet, Hazrat Nizamuddin said: once there was a companion sitting with a group of people. He heard someone behind him say twice or thrice that he heard it from the Prophet that on such and such day, he happened to be at such and such place and Abu Bakr and Umar were with him. That companion of the Prophet looked around and saw that it was Amirul Mu'minin Ali who was saying this. Hazrat Nizamuddin wanted to tell his disciples how just and considerate the companions of the Prophet were for each other.[16] The bonding between them was best expressed by Umar's unique desire to be a curl of hair on Abu Bakr's chest (*aye kaash man yak taar-i muyi boodami bar sineh-ye abu bakr*).[17]

Hazrat Nizamuddin often lamented that such fine people were rare in his time, though some Sufis were still striving to meet certain levels of excellence in ethical standards. They kept themselves away from the materialistic attachments of the world to emerge as men of excellence and piety. Without the distance from the materialistic allurements of the world, the recognition of their excellence would not be enduring. In view of the worldliness and materialism all around, the Sufis liked to follow the Prophet's statement that poverty was a matter of pride for him. Poetically articulating the need for studied distance from lust and desires, Hazrat Nizamuddin once recited this couplet:

Ta paak na-gardi be-tu aatish na-dehand
Ta khaak na-gardi be-tu aabash ne-dehand

Until purged of the impurities, the flame of love
will not be kindled
Until humbled like earth, your soil of hope will
not be watered.[18]

12

ATTITUDE TOWARDS CONVERSION AND ISLAMICIZATION

No amount of force can change the heart of the people, but the blessed company of a pious Muslim can possibly transform a non-Muslim into a pious Muslim. The real problem with Islam is the lack of integrity in Muslims themselves.

– Hazrat Nizamuddin Auliya, as quoted in *Fawa'id-ul-Fu'ad*

This chapter looks at the question of conversion and Islamicization in the Indian environment and Hazrat Nizamuddin Auliya's opinion on the matter. The missionary and proselytizing activities of the Sufis and their organizations have been noted in some modern writings.[1] Some scholars have also highlighted the significance of miraculous combats between the Sufis and non-Muslim miracle workers reported in Sufi literature, yet several dimensions of the details of these contests require further elaboration.[2] This chapter will analyse some relevant anecdotes, revealing the attitude of Chishti Sufis, particularly Nizamuddin Auliya's, towards non-Muslim spiritual power-holders.

As we have seen, Nizamuddin was trying to educate the followers in the Sufi way of cultivating the heart for the love of God, which was expressed through service to humanity, which was considered to be the best form of prayers. Like his Chishti predecessors, he presented a tolerant and peaceful vision of Islam, one that sought to draw non-Muslims without force or political power. This ensured they thrived in a spiritually competitive landscape and attracted followers across the Indian subcontinent, with or without conversion. While Sufis were not opposed to conversion, they believed that moral reform within the Muslim community was more urgent than winning new converts. Over time, as historians note, many non-Muslims did embrace Islam through the gradual cultural influence of Sufis, particularly in regions such as Punjab, the Deccan and Bengal.

Once, Nizamuddin was introduced to a Hindu visitor brought to him for the purpose of conversion. Instead of simply offering him the Islamic formula of faith in one God (Allah) and Muhammad being His Prophet, Nizamuddin gave an emotional lecture on the need to cultivate the heart to become a good Muslim rather than forcing non-Muslims into Islam as a mere matter of formality. This point is illustrated with the story of the arrest of the king of Iraq after the Arab conquest under the second caliph, Umar al-Khattab. The king refused to convert to Islam even on pain of death, but soon the company of a sincere practising Muslim of the Sufi kind transformed his heart, so that he offered to embrace Islam. The concluding anecdote shows how a Jewish neighbour of a prominent Sufi observed that the latter was creating a model of Islam that was difficult to achieve, and at the same time, the general conduct of Muslims appeared repulsive. Conversion to Islam of this kind was considered meaningless. The full details of the text are instructive and make for interesting reading.

One of the disciples, a slave, arrived with a

Hindu and said that this was his brother. When both were seated, Nizamuddin asked the slave whether his brother had any inclination towards Islam. He replied that it was precisely for this purpose that he had brought him to his service so that, by the blessing of his glance, he might become a Muslim (*musalman shawad*). With tears in his eyes, Nizamuddin remarked that no matter what one says, one cannot change the hearts of these people (*qaum*), but one can hope that through the grace of the company of a pious person, they might become Muslim. After this, he narrated the following anecdote. When Umar Khattab acceded to the caliphate, there was a battle with the king of Iraq in which the king was captured and brought to the presence of Umar. He was told that if he became a Muslim, the country of Iraq would be granted to him. The king said he would not embrace Islam. Umar commanded him to choose Islam or the sword (*imma al-islam wa imma al-sayf*); if he did not accept Islam, he would be killed. The king declared, 'Kill me; I will not accept Islam' (*Be-kush man islam qabul na mi-kunam*). Umar ordered his attendants to bring the sword and call the executioner.

That king was very clever and wise. Observing the situation, he turned to Umar and requested some water, as he was thirsty. Umar ordered to bring water, and it was brought in a glass vessel. The king submitted that he would not drink water from that vessel. Umar commanded that since he had been a king, water be brought for him in gold and silver vessels, which was complied with. The king refused again; he asked for water to be brought in a vessel of clay. A clay pot was filled with water and handed over to him. Turning his face towards Umar, he asked him to pledge that he would not be killed till he had drunk the water from that earthen pot. Umar agreed. The king then threw the pot on the ground; the pot broke, and the water spilled. Then, he told Umar that, since he did not drink the water from the pot, he should follow his promise not to kill him, and he should be pardoned now. Amazed at his sagacity, Umar agreed to offer amnesty to him. He was then entrusted to the company of a friend, who was an extremely capable and pious ascetic.

The king of Iraq was taken to the house of that friend. Soon, the company of the virtuous host made such an impact on him that he sent a message to Umar that he might be summoned to his presence to profess his faith in Islam. Umar invited him and offered Islam (*talbid wa islam 'arz kard*), and the king became a Muslim (*u musalman shud*). When he had embraced Islam (*chun islam awarad*), Umar said he would now offer the governorship of Iraq to him. The king replied that the governorship was of no use to him; instead, he might be given a village in the country of Iraq, which should be adequate for his subsistence. When Umar agreed, the king requested that he should be granted a desolate village (*dehi kharab*) so that he could work to make it habitable (*abadan kunam*). Umar sent some people to the region of Iraq. They searched all over the country, but could not find a single village that was in ruins. Umar apprised the king of the situation that not a single village in Iraq was uninhabited. The king replied that his intention was to confirm that he had handed over a prosperous Iraq to him, and that he would be held answerable on the Day of Judgement (*qayamat*) if a single village were deserted. Recounting this anecdote (*hikayat*) with tears in his eyes, Hazrat Nizamuddin was full of praise for the sagacity and ingeniousness of the king.

Commenting on the integrity and honesty of Islam and Muslims (*sidaq o dayanat*), Nizamuddin narrated the story of a Jew who lived in the neighbourhood of Khwaja Bayazid Bustami. When Bayazid passed away, the Jew, who, like others, was mourning, was asked why he did not become a

Muslim (*chera musalman na mi-shawi*). The Jew asked what kind of Muslim they wanted him to become, adding that if Islam was what Bayazid practised, he would not be able to attain it and if it were what they (Muslims) have, he was ashamed of it (*ma ra az in islam 'ar mi-ayad*). Transformation of the heart, rather than direct conversion, forcible or otherwise, was the recommended ideal, insofar as the virtue of being a sincere Muslim was concerned – which in other words meant a good human being.

Thus, Nizamuddin himself refused to convert any non-Muslims to Islam but narrated interesting anecdotes on the matter. The tales involved miraculous encounters, not necessarily leading to conversion in all cases, but illustrating the spiritual superiority of the Sufi fraternity. Such stories were part of a large corpus of Sufi literature, from which they were recounted with modifications, depending on individuals and contexts. For instance, an earlier version of the anecdote of the conversion of a Jew at the hands of Khwaja Fuzail Ayaz, recorded in a so-called 'spurious' *malfuzat* of Nizamuddin Auliya, can be found in Awfi's *Jawama-ul-Hikayat*, completed sometime after 1230. Thus, classification of the texts as 'authentic' and 'spurious' is superficial, as both are suffused with amusing tales of miracles which may indeed sound irrational to the 'modern' mind.[3] What is important and relevant is the purpose of and the context in which these miraculous conversion stories and miracles were generally narrated. As Caroline Bynum says, though, in a different context, that these accounts 'tell us of objects and events carefully constructed to elicit awe, delight, and dread'.[4] Further, the accounts of competition in 'displays of power and splendour' included 'intricate tricks and automata, calculated to amaze and tantalise'.[5]

There is a general belief in a dominant historiographical tradition that early mystic records did not refer to a single case of conversion.[6] However, the Chishti texts of the Delhi Sultanate present the image of Sufi saints as the primary agent for proselytization and propagation of Islam. Sufi shaikhs such as Muinuddin Chishti, Jalaluddin Tabrezi,[7] Fariduddin Ganj-i-Shakar, Qutbuddin Bakhtiyar Kaki and Saiyid Ashraf Jahangir Simnani[8] are portrayed as the chief propagators of Islam in North India. Caste oppression and the drawing capability that egalitarian Islam might have,[9] or, for that matter, economic and political dimensions, are not mentioned in the literature of the period as factors for conversion. The one recurrent motive for the conversion of individuals and at times of the entire locality or town is the attraction to the miracle-working shaikh. Most cases of mass conversion are shown to be the outcome of oppositional encounters of the visiting shaikh with the local holy man, generally a *yogi,* in full view of the public, in which the former emerges victorious and establishes his authority.

The accounts of conversion are generally the sequel to the outcome of the contests involving the visiting shaikh and a local challenger or *yogi* visiting the *jama'at-khana* of the shaikh to test his spiritual accomplishments; or the shaikh's thaumaturgic role, such as his revival of the dead and protection from malevolent supernatural beings. We may refer to two episodes of conversion reportedly narrated by Nizamuddin Auliya.

The first, Khwaja Fuzail Ayaz, was a dacoit before he turned to the mystic way of life. Repenting his misdeeds, he called all those who were robbed by him and sought their forgiveness by returning their belongings. Among them was a Jew who was not willing to forgive the shaikh. He would be convinced of his sincerity only if the shaikh succeeded in producing gold from the ground beneath his feet. The shaikh immediately performed the miraculous feat to the satisfaction of the Jew, who, after that, converted to Islam. He then informed the shaikh that it was mentioned in the Jewish scriptures that those whose repentance was accepted by God were blessed with the power of converting soil into gold. He added that by asking the shaikh to do so, he only wanted the confirmation that his repentance had been accepted.[10] An earlier version of this anecdote was recorded in an early thirteenth-century Persian text, Awfi's *Jawama-ul-Hikayat,* which discounts the view that such anecdotes had suddenly sprung up in the middle of the fourteenth century.[11]

The second anecdote was of a Jewish neighbour of Khwaja Bayazid Bustami, as recorded in the *Tazkirat-ul-Auliya*. Once, when he was out of town, his wife gave birth to a child. The lady had no means to arrange for a lamp in the house. The infant kept crying in the darkness. When the shaikh came to know of it, he started purchasing oil every day from the grocer next door for the Jewish lady. When the Jew returned home from his long sojourn, his wife informed him of the shaikh's kind gesture. The Jew was impressed and went to visit the shaikh to express his gratitude. The shaikh remarked that he was only fulfilling his duty towards a neighbour. Moved, the Jew also accepted the Islamic faith.[12]

In the above mentioned anecdotes and other

stories, the emphasis is on establishing the superiority of the Sufi shaikh. The opponents fall at the feet of the shaikh in full view of the public and announce their acceptance of the superior miraculous ability of the shaikh. The name that the shaikh gives him after his conversion further confirms the inferiority of the antagonist. He is generally named as Abdullah – the servant of God. It is only after prolonged and rigorous meditation (*mujahida*) that the status of *waliullah,* that is, the friend of God, is conferred on him. In a particular case, however, a saintly Hindu of Nagaur was accorded the status of a *wali* even before his conversion. While remarking that if a *kafir* (infidel) had faith at the time of his death, he would be treated by God as a *mu'min* (believer), Nizamuddin Auliya told his audience that Hamiduddin Nagauri would often call a Hindu of Nagaur as a *wali* of God.[13] Amir Khwurd added that the shaikh used to say that the Hindu, whom he called a *wali,* would die as a faithful.[14] Later, Shaikh Jamali went one step further. According to him, the people wondered when the shaikh called an infidel a friend of God. As it turned out, he converted to Islam and joined the ranks of the saints.[15] Thus, the prophecy of the shaikh proved to be true, and Amir Khwurd and Jamali confirmed his omniscience.

Further, literature records the tale of the conversion of a dacoit at the hands of Jalaluddin Tabrezi. Fariduddin Ganj-i-Shakar had narrated the incident. Nizamuddin recounted another story in which Tabrezi was said to have converted the entire Hindu population of a town in Hindustan. It is recorded that Tabrezi reached a town where a demon (*div*) used to eat a person each night. The shaikh captured the *div* and put it in a vessel. The entire populace embraced Islam as a consequence.[16] Apart from this, there are many such descriptions in the texts in which the Sufi shaikhs are shown to be protecting hapless people from the clutches of the evil spirits. It is to be noted, however, that in most cases the victims were perhaps Muslims, for we find that the shaikh recommended the recital of specific passages from the Qur'an as protection against the possible attack from the demon and other supernatural beings such as the *pari*.

Certain general inferences can perhaps be drawn from the anecdotes in Sufi literature, especially referring to Hazrat Nizamuddin. The notion that the Chishtis were completely disinterested in conversion is not supported by the texts. In all stories of conversion, the decisive factor was the superior miraculous ability of the shaikh. The shaikh's power to revive the dead, his ability to discover a thief or a *kafir* and his victory in oppositional encounters, both at the time of his arrival in a non-Muslim environment or with a visiting Hindu holy man in the *jama'at-khana*, led to the acceptance of the charisma of the shaikh both by the opponent and others who were witness to it. The subsequent conversion at the hands of the shaikh brought him immense prestige and authority in his *wilayat*. Thus, the popularity of the shaikh depended on the public display of miracles. The narration of the accounts of miraculous conversion by the shaikhs in their *jama'at-khana*s with the appended laudatory comments helped in their further perpetuation among the followers and the general populace.[17]

This is further supported by the evidence that much before the works of the so-called 'propagandists', Amir Hasan, Amir Khusrau and Ziyauddin Barani, had become known,[18] the Chishti shaikhs enjoyed widespread popularity, so much so that the word of mouth accounts began to be put down on paper and sometimes the authorship of such popular literature was attributed to the shaikh himself, providing it a veneer of authenticity. A disciple informed Nizamuddin Auliya that a person in Awadh had shown him a book which was supposed to have been written by him (the shaikh), which the shaikh denied.[19] Later, Chiragh-i-Dehli quoted this statement during a discussion in his *jama'at-khana* and also suggested that the *malfuzat* of Chishti predecessors such as 'Usman Harwani and Qutbuddin Bakhtiyar Kaki, which were in circulation in Sufi circles, were not known in the time of Nizamuddin Auliya; otherwise, he would have referred to them.[20] Modern scholars use the two pieces of evidence to reject several *malfuzat* collections, including the one compiled by Nizamuddin Auliya as 'spurious'. They, however, ignore the point that there was a difference between writing a book and compiling *malfuzat* of the *pir* (a Sufi guide). Moreover, they set aside Nizamuddin's statement that he had also collected some *malfuzat* of his *pir,* Fariduddin Ganj-i-Shakar, and that they were in his possession at the time of the compilation of his own discourses, *Fawa'id-ul-Fu'ad.*[21]

In these conversations, the attitude towards conversion and ways and means to achieve it differed from one shaikh to another within the Chishti *silsila.* Although Nizamuddin Auliya has narrated the accounts of the sudden transformation of individuals and groups on account of the charisma of the shaikh, he instead preferred a gradual change of heart of a person in the company of a righteous Muslim. Earlier, Fariduddin Ganj-i-Shakar extolled the unmatched miraculous ability of his Chishti predecessors to convert non-Muslims, and he reportedly forced some visiting *yogis* to enter the fold.

We do not intend here to establish the historicity of the accounts of miraculous conversion in the Sufi literature. But, if the anecdotes of the confrontation between the shaikhs and non-Muslim religious leaders are to be dismissed as fake – though we must remember that they are also recorded in the 'authentic' *malfuzat* collections – then at least they are useful for the diverse images they portray of non-Muslims in Sufi circles of the period. Ideology-driven histories have not been able to do justice to this fascinating literature on the Sufis' crucial presence in the medieval Indian environment. A proper appreciation of this important strand of Islamic tradition can help understand why Sufi *dargahs* have continued to attract a large number of non-Muslim devotees even in the times of Islamophobia and terrorism. The emphasis was on kindness and empathy rather than forcibly bringing converts to Islam. No wonder then that a large majority of visitors to Sufi shrines are non-Muslims, seeking blessings and benediction.

13

EXCELLENCE OF DISCIPLES

Blind devotion of a *murid* (disciple) to a Sufi *pir* (master) is recommended, but the latter is known by his disciples. No amount of claims of being a preceptor by a Sufi master is enough, unless disciples themselves recognize the master as such.

– Hazrat Nizamuddin Auliya on *piri–muridi* relationship, as quoted in *Fawa'id-ul-Fu'ad*

Hazrat Nizamuddin Auliya's large circles of companions, friends and disciples had acquired virtues which made them exceptional in terms of their excellence. When they came to meet him for the first time, he was not judging them for who they were, but for who they would become after joining his discipleship. The medieval Sufi biographies sing praises of the highest qualities of a large number of mystic-like poets, writers, historians and intellectuals associated with Hazrat Nizamuddin. These include the most famous and closest of disciples, Sufi poet Amir Khusrau, Sufi poet Amir Hasan Sijzi, who shot to fame with his meticulously prepared collection of spiritual conversations of Hazrat Nizamuddin in his life time, Khwaja Ziyauddin Barani, who grew out of his role as a personal adviser of Sultan Muhammad Tughlaq to emerge late in his life as a political ideologue and historian par excellence, and Amir Khwurd Kirmani whose celebration of the Chishti tradition through a voluminous collection of biographies of Sufi saints, *Siyar-ul-Auliya*, went a long way in transmitting the tradition far and wide and in posterity in all its excellence.

Numerous other disciples of Hazrat Nizamuddin excelled in their own enigmatic ways. Several of them spread to different parts of the subcontinent. Their followers, in turn, spread Hazrat Nizamuddin's teachings further, creating a spiritual geography, which made him and other leading Chishti masters a part of the lasting and glorious tradition of the subcontinental scale. This chapter is focused on discussing the superlative talents of some of the close associates of Hazrat Nizamuddin. Their contributions to the building of this tradition of spiritual excellence are considered immense.

Hazrat Amir Khusrau

Amir Khusrau's name is invariably mentioned in every Sufi *qawwali* programme. His name and his versatile contributions to the glorious history of achievements and excellence of India's cultural heritage, especially music and poetry, are discussed along with the contributions of other notable stalwarts of the first Chishti order. Nevertheless, historians have written very little on Khusrau's life and works, although he had seen the power struggles, political alliances, battles and rebellions in the Delhi Sultanate closely and had glorified the achievements of the sultans with much enthusiasm. Modern Persian and Urdu scholars have praised Khusrau's abilities, but good research works on him are rare. A huge treasure of Khusrau's writings is preserved in the form of manuscripts, but there is a need to continue their preservation, publication and study from linguistic and historical perspectives.[1]

Medieval Sufi authors have emphasized the

value of Khusrau's credentials as a Sufi poet, closely trained by Hazrat Nizamuddin Auliya.[2] Describing him as the sultan of poets, a great scholar and a wonderful poet, Abdul Haq Muhaddis Dehlawi had said that Khusrau was one of the old friends and disciples of Nizamuddin Auliya. He had immense respect and love for the shaikh, and the latter also showered great affection and favour on him. No one else had such confidentiality and closeness with Hazrat Nizamuddin as Amir Khusrau had. It was his habit to always appear in the service of the shaikh after the night prayer (*Isha*) and, apart from all kinds of conversation, he would present the requests of his friends. One such request was from Nasiruddin Chiragh-i-Dehli seeking closer attention and training, which eventually made him Nizamuddin's chief successor in the Chishti order.

Abdul Haq further said that Hazrat Nizamuddin trained Amir Khusrau in Sufi spirituality by writing letters to him, addressing him as Turk-Allah (Turk of God). The content of one letter sums up the teachings of Chishti Sufis in a wonderful advice: after protecting the body, one should refrain from all conducts which are forbidden according to the *shari'at* and one should keep an eye on one's behaviour at all times; one's precious life should be considered a blessing because due to it all legitimate expectations are achieved; life should not be wasted in useless activities; and if the bodily desires are overwhelming, it should be transformed into a cheerful exhilaration of the heart, because this is what is trusted in the Sufi path (*tariqat*), and the desire for goodness should be kept above everything else. Thus, according to Abdul Haq, Khusrau was fully aware of the principles of Sufism and the condition of dervishes. He had relations with courtiers and kings, but, naturally, his heart was not tainted with the moral bankruptcy of the ruling people. The spiritual blessings of the kind found in Khusrau's poetry are rarely available in the compositions of the sinners.[3]

It was the impact of the Sufi–Islamic upbringing of this poet, who was born in a political aristocratic family connected to the Delhi Sultanate (father was a Turk and mother a Rajput), that Khusrau used to recite seven out of thirty sections of the Qur'an every night in the late-night prayers (*Tahajjud*). No wonder Hazrat Nizamuddin used to start the *mahlfil-i-sama* in his hospice with Khusrau's recitation of the Qur'an. One day, the shaikh asked him: 'Turk, what is the state of your spiritual activities?' Khusrau said, 'Sir (*Makhdum*), the last part of the night is mostly spent in remembering God and weeping due to overwhelming emotions (remembering Him).' The shaikh liked this reply and remarked: 'Praise be to God (*Alhamdulillah*)'; his spiritual training under Nizamuddin was becoming visible.[4]

In his Persian poetry of love, Khusrau adopted the Iranian–Isfahani style on the advice of his Hazrat Nizamuddin. The shaikh had gifted him a special cap with his own hands and advised him to always keep in mind the sayings and ways of the Sufis. Khusrau was continually compared with great Iranian poets such as Sadi, Hafiz and Nasir Khusrau. According to an early report, a dervish completely immersed in the remembrance of God had predicted at the time of Khusrau's birth that this lucky and talented child would go two steps ahead of the Persian poet Khaqani.[5] Abdul Haq had said that perhaps this meant Khusrau's mastery in poetic forms such as *masnavi* and *ghazal*, because he could not reach Khaqani's level in poetry of praise (*qasida*). In this way, in poetry, he was equal to Khaqani but could not surpass him.[6]

As mentioned above, Amir Khusrau's name is much celebrated in the history of Indian, Persian and musical traditions. Regarding Khusrau's excellent *ghazals*, his modern biographer Waheed Mirza writes: 'The soul and grace of Khusrau's ghazals is evident from the fact that more than six hundred years have passed since his time, but in sama and qawwali gatherings, his ghazals are probably still the most popular and prevalent.' The biggest tribute to Khusrau's excellence as a poet and writer came from Hazrat Nizamuddin himself. The saint announced that there was no one equal to Amir Khusrau in poetry and prose; the kingship of poetry is his exclusive domain. This is our Khusrau, not Nasir Khusrau (an Iranian poet):

Khusrau ke be-nazm o nasr misalash kam khwaast
Milkiyat o mulk-i sukhan aan khusrau raast
In khusrau maast nasir khusrau nist
Zira keh khudaye nasir-i khusrau maast

There were few like Khusrau in poetry and prose;
The kingdom of the country of poetry belongs to Khusrau.
This Khusrau is ours, not Nasir Khusrau;
and God is the helper of our Khusrau.[7]

The close relation between the saint and the disciple was eventually seen in lasting terms when Amir Khusrau bitterly mourned and lamented the loss of Hazrat Nizamuddin when he passed away in 1325. Khusrau himself did not survive for more than six months and was buried in proximity to Hazrat Nizamuddin's grave. Khusrau's Hindi verses mourning Nizamuddin's death became a part of the Sufi tradition's folk memory:

Gori sowe sej par mukh par daare kes
Chal khusrau ghar aapne rayn bhai chahun des

The pretty one sleeps on the bed with hair spread on his face;
Khusrau go home, the darkness of night has engulfed all around.

Writing thirty years later, and calling himself a friend of Amir Khusrau, Ziyauddin Barani noted that Amir Khusrau was the king of poets and had no rival in inventing subtleties of meaning, authoring a large number of books and unveiling the pleasures of hidden meanings. According to Barani, if other masters of the art, experts of prose and poetry, excelled in one or two branches of learning, Amir Khusrau was distinguished and eminent in all branches of knowledge. He added that such a multi-talented and versatile person, who was outstanding in all genres of poetry, had never been seen in the past.[8]

Drawing attention to Amir Khusrau's close and faithful association with Hazrat Nizamuddin Auliya as one of his main disciples, Barani writes that with all the accomplishments and excellence in various sciences, he was a perfect Sufi. Most of his life was spent in fasting and praying. He continually kept a fast and spent his time in devotions both for himself and for benefiting others. Sunk in divine love, Khusrau was deeply given to Sufi music (*sama*) and was a man of ecstasy. He achieved great excellence in the art of singing and composing music. Barani concluded his portrait of Khusrau as one of the wonders of the reign of Sultan Alauddin Khalji by asserting how all the qualities which can be attributed to a fine and balanced temperament were given to him in perfection, who shone like a peerless being.[9]

Amir Hasan Sijzi

Amir Hasan was born in a family that relocated from Sistan in Iran to work as top military officials and bureaucrats in the service of the Delhi sultans in the thirteenth century. The Sistani advance guards in the service of Ghiyasuddin Balban (ruled 1266–86) created quite a spectacle with their shining silver sabres, as mentioned by Ziyauddin Barani in his *Tarikh-i-Firuz Shahi*. Barani, writing in the middle of the fourteenth century, had counted Amir Hasan Sijzi and Amir Khusrau as common friends, though he was much younger than they were. We shall return to Barani's observations later in this chapter, but Amir Hasan and Amir Khusrau were indeed close associates in Sultanate service as fine poets and eminent disciples of Hazrat Nizamuddin Auliya.

Writing in the late sixteenth and early seventeenth century, Abdul Haq Muhaddis Dehlawi has included a biographical sketch of Amir Hasan immediately after that of Amir Khusrau in his famous book on the lives of the Sufis, *Akhbar-ul-Akhyar*. Amir Hasan is presented as a distinguished scholar of his time, who enjoyed considerable respect among his peers. Because of the closeness and kind favours of Hazrat Nizamuddin, he was considered superior and distinct among his disciples.[10] On account of his giving up on the rough life of a sinner, having a cleansed inner self and all other fine tributes expected from the illustrious disciples of Hazrat Nizamuddin, he was blessed with all the distinguished features of Islamic mysticism (*tasawwuf*). In terms of excellence as a poet, his friend Khusrau enjoyed much popularity in Sufi *qawwali* circles, but Amir Hasan had an advantage of sorts over the former, because he wrote eulogies (*qasida*: poetry of praise) for Sultan Ghiyasuddin Balban. Khusrau, on the other hand, wrote in celebration of the extraordinary talents of Balban's son, Khan-i-Shahid, the governor of Multan, who died fighting the Mongols during one of their many raids in the thirteenth century.

Amir Hasan also became famous for his collection of the discourses of Hazrat Nizamuddin, *Fawa'id-ul-Fu'ad*, which, for its fine expositions and meanings of mystical concepts and experiences, became a veritable guidebook for Hazrat Nizamuddin's associates and followers. In this text, Amir Hasan also noted his own presence by announcing at the beginning of each chapter, called *majlis* (assembly), that he had the honour of kissing the feet of the saint on such and such day of a particular month of a particular year, covering a period of fifteen years. Hasan also frequently mentioned his own participation through recitation of some poetical compositions of his own and of other poets on the current topics of conversation in Hazrat Nizamuddin's hospice. His experiences while reciting the Qur'an or listening to Sufi *qawwali* or narration of his dreams were appreciatively heard by the saint.

Amir Khusrau is reported to have expressed his

wish to make Amir Hasan credit the compilation of *Fawa'id-ul-Fu'ad* to Khusrau, in exchange for which the credit for all his poetic collections will be given to Hasan.[11] This once again showed Khusrau's devotion to Hazrat Nizamuddin and the value of his spiritual conversations (*malfuzat*) collected in *Fawa'id-ul-Fu'ad*. Khusrau's own small collection of Hazrat Nizamuddin's discourses, *Afzal-ul-Fawa'id*, is not considered to be of the same value as *Fawa'id-ul-Fu'ad* since the time of its publicly known compilation early in the fourteenth century. Also, as an accomplished poet and a devotee of Nizamuddin Auliya, Amir Hasan could not have agreed to Amir Khusrau's proposal for exchange of credits for their work, even on pain of death or lure of gold for that matter.

The life of the officials under Sultan Alauddin Khalji could lead to sustained periods of financial embarrassment. Nasiruddin Chiragh-i-Dehli had later pointed out that things were cheap because of the sultan's market reform. For instance, one *man* (a mound of nearly 40 kilograms) of watermelon was available for just a *tinka* (a coin of small value), but who could afford to spend a *tinka*?

In such difficult times, when he could almost be wasting his life, association with Hazrat Nizamuddin brought a lot of peace to Amir Hasan's disturbed mind. His life earlier, full of wine and poetry, was not enough for spiritual solace. Repentant, he joined the circle of Nizamuddin as a disciple, and the saint was clairvoyant in recognizing the fine qualities of Amir Hasan as he earlier did with Khusrau and many others. There was no background check of persons wishing to seek an audience with Nizamuddin Auliya and become a disciple. Subsequent spiritual progress of the person depended on his interest and determination. It is related that once visiting the house of Hazrat Nizamuddin, Amir Hasan found the saint sitting on the stairs with a strong breeze repeatedly shutting the door. Amir Hasan decided to stand there holding the door to ensure it was not moving or closing. Noticing that Amir Hasan was holding the door to keep it open, Hazrat Nizamuddin asked why he was not letting the door move. Hasan replied that he was now holding on to this particular door (of hope for blessings and salvation). Impressed, Nizamuddin remarked that he (Hasan) was indeed holding the door and doing it strongly.[12]

Strong commitment to discipleship, bordering on blind faith, is the recommended ideal in *piri–muridi* or the disciple–master relationship in Sufism. At the same time, it was recognized that the claims over disciples by a Sufi were nothing, unless and until disciples themselves professed their veneration for their spiritual master. A related anecdote mentions Amir Hasan quoting Malih, a former slave and friend who had also joined the discipleship of Hazrat Nizamuddin Auliya, as saying that the *hajj* was a recommended practice for someone who did not have a *pir*. Emotionally overwhelmed and weeping over the above remark, Nizamuddin recited this line from a Persian couplet:

> *In rah be-suye ka'ba rawad, aan be-suye doost*
>
> This road goes to the ka'ba, and that to the friend.[13]

Amir Hasan also participated in the acrimonious debate on Sufi music and criticized those who opposed it. He also confessed to Nizamuddin that sometimes the pleasure and relief he got in listening to Sufi music was immense, not comparable to other forms of prayer.[14] After the passing away of both Hazrat Nizamuddin and Amir Khusrau and the taking over of the power of the Sultanate by the despotic ruler Muhammad Tughlaq, all within months in the fateful year of 1325, life in Delhi was going to be difficult. The Tughlaq sultan had forced large sections of the notables to move to Daulatabad (Deogiri) in the Deccan. Some resisted the sultan's order, as did Nasiruddin Chiragh-i-Dehli; others could not. The sultan is known to have also used his own mother to portray the seriousness of his project of shifting the capital to Daulatabad, making her undertake a hazardous journey to a regional centre that was not fully conquered. When the plan did not work to the ruler's satisfaction, he issued a general statement to the effect that those who were forcibly displaced and wanted to return to Delhi could do so. Amir Hasan, who had also moved to Daulatabad, preferred to stay back and became well known there as Amir Hasan Dehlawi.

Ziyauddin Barani penned a fine tribute to the latter as well. His portrayal of Khusrau's extraordinary qualities has been noted in the previous section. Barani wrote, besides Khusrau, the other incomparable poet of the age was Amir Hasan, with many compilations of prose and poetry to his credit. In the beauty of construction and flow of style, he was an accomplished master. There are several collections of his poetry as well as some treatises in prose. For his immense felicity and flow in *ghazal*, poetry of love, he was called the Sa'di of

Hindustan.[15] Barani further noted that the laudable character with subtle expression, witty humour, a wonderful ability to recall annals and anecdotes of kings, elders and scholars of Delhi, constancy of intellect and opinions, always holding fast to contentment, purity of faith, leading a happy life without worldly resources, and detachment from the world like a true Sufi were some of the exceptional qualities of Amir Hasan. Due to the intense faith he had in Hazrat Nizamuddin Auliya, he compiled his conversations in *Fawa'id-ul-Fu'ad*, which became the guidebook for faithful Sufis.[16] Barani concluded that Amir Hasan was endowed with such an agreeable character and fine attributes – lively, sweet-tongued, witty, pleasant, civilized, refined and sensitive to the temperaments of others – that the pleasure and comfort in his company was incomparable.[17]

Through the large numbers of pages in the voluminous *Fawa'id-ul-Fu'ad*, Amir Hasan presented Hazrat Nizamuddin and his association with him in the finest imaginable terms. Hasan continually kept emphasizing the value of the kindness and generosity of the saint, which sort of reformed him spiritually and kept him going in his difficult times. Addressing Hazrat Nizamuddin as the sultan among the friends of God, Qutb of the world, king of mystics and gnostics, foundation of truth and faith from his given name, Amir Hasan wrote in the preface of the fifth and last volume of *Faw'id-ul-Fu'ad* that Nizamuddin was the chosen seal of the Sufis, just as Prophet Muhammad was the last of the Prophets:

Yaki az ummat khatam-ul-nabiyyin
Na-shud juzwi kasi khatam-ul-masha'ikh

One among the followers of Prophet Muhammad
No one else is the seal of the Sufis, except him.[18]

Khwaja Ziyauddin Barani

If I say that there does not exist in the world
Any other book like the history of mine
Since there is none who is proficient in this science
Who will believe what I say.

– Khwaja Ziyauddin Barani in the Introduction to his *Tarikh-i-Firuz Shahi*[19]

Historian, political theorist and close associate of Sultan Muhammad Tughlaq for close to two decades, Khwaja Ziyauddin Barani was also a close friend of Amir Khusrau and Amir Hasan Sijzi and, together with them, a companion of Hazrat Nizamuddin Auliya as well. In his last years, when he was removed from the court of Sultan Firuz Shah Tughlaq (ruled 1351–1388), Barani transformed himself into an eminent author who had withdrawn from the world and took refuge in the tomb complex of Hazrat Nizamuddin. He was buried in Nizamuddin's *dargah* after passing away, very much like a Sufi *buzurg* and *faqir* (saintly old man). As Amir Khwurd notes, Barani left for the eternal world in a style that was typically Sufi, *mardana* and *ashiqana*.[20] Amir Khwurd also mentions that Barani himself had withdrawn from politics with a small pension of sorts for his daily creature comforts from Sultan Firuz Shah. This withdrawal is credited to Barani's association with Hazrat Nizamuddin and memories attached to him, and thus, eventually, spiritual sacrifices prevailed over worldly comforts gained from the political domain. He had no money when he died, but had devoted his time to quickly bring out several books which have survived and made Barani famous to posterity.[21]

Ziyaudin Barani's *Tarikh-i-Firuz Shahi* and *Fatawa-i-Jahandari* are two well-known texts of history and political theory, without which political history of the Delhi Sultanate would have been much poor. Barani also wrote several other books, of whom the most important is the biography of the Prophet, *Sanai Muhammadi*, and also exceptionally an autobiographical text called *Hasrat-nama*, or an account of unfulfilled desires, which is available in only some fragments now. Barani's *Tarikh-i-Firuz Shahi* is particularly important for our purpose here as he has recorded details of tremendous influence of Hazrat Nizamuddin Auliya in the public life of the city of Delhi, especially in Sufi mystical devotion and Islamic religiosity. This was the time when Sultan Alauddin Khalji was ruling with a heavy hand, and Nizamuddin had very intelligently maintained a studied distance from matters political. Amir Khusrau and Amir Hasan Sijzi, along with Barani and several other disciples, could have served as a bridge between the sultan and the Sufi.

Barani writes that the royal capital of Delhi, especially in the last ten years of the reign of Sultan Alauddin Khalji, witnessed the blessed presence of three eminent saints: Shaikhul Islam Nizamuddin, Shaikhul Islam Alauddin and Shaikhul Islam Ruknuddin. They illuminated the public culture of the great city, making it a source of envy for Baghdad, a cause of jealousy for Cairo, equal to

Constantinople, and comparable to Baitul Muqaddas, Jerusalem. Under the influence of the three peerless and exceptional personages, a large number of people took recourse to repentance, becoming their disciples and followers and abandoning sins and impiety. They became deeply drawn to prayers, both obligatory for their own well-being (*ibadat-i-lazima*) and for the benefit of others, as a matter of kindness (*ibadat-i-mutaddia*). The material greed of the world, which causes the undoing of devotions and good acts of human beings, was weakened in the hearts of the people due to the nobility of character, sublime attributes as well as the attitude of renunciation and rejection of the world by those saints, who served as the vice regent of the Prophethood. Their influence ensured men learned the virtues of honesty in their dealings, and sincere concerns for austerities and abstinence changed their hearts to make them better human beings. Prayers, recitation of religious formulae, submission to the will of God, wish for mystical inspiration, etc., occupied their inner self.[22]

Severe punishments to the corrupt people in government service or in the bazars by Alauddin Khalji had created terror in the minds of the people. People were being violently compelled to lead an honest public life. At this time, Hazrat Nizamuddin had thrown open the gates of his hospice for large numbers of people to become his disciples, not discriminating between elite or plebian, rich or poor, king or pauper, educated or ignorant, gentleman or rustic, townsman or villager and free or slave. The discipleship of the shaikh meant that they were expected to lead a clean life, having repented from the life of a sinner. In some cases, the discipleship needed renewal as people were not always able to maintain the oath and commitment for a pietistic life. The masses became inclined both by faith and by emulating the example of Hazrat Nizamuddin towards acts of devotion and worship (*namaz*, recitation of Qur'an, *zikr*, and chanting of other kinds of recommended mantras). *Namaz*, obligatory or recommended, in congregation or private, especially became a marker of widespread religiosity, which, in turn, protected people from evil acts.[23]

Barani further writes that he personally knew many disciples of Hazrat Nizamuddin Auliya, who had attained the status of having acquired paranormal abilities (*kashf* and *karamat*) due to his rigorous training and influence, going beyond the normal requirement of religious practices to lead a pious life. Students or members of the elite society, who had associated with Hazrat Nizamuddin, were found to have developed an interest in acquiring and reading books on Sufism. There appeared many buyers of many classic treatises on Islam and mysticism such as *Qut-ul-Qulub* of Abu Talib Makki (died 996), *Ihya-ul-Ulum* of Ghazali (died 1111), *Awarif-ul-Ma'arif* of Shaikh Shahabuddin Suhrawardi (died 1234), *Kashf-ul-Mahjub* of Shaikh Ali Hujwiri Dataganj Bakhsh of Lahore (died 1074), *Risala-i-Qushair* of Abul Qasim Abdul Karim Qushairi (died 1072), *Mirsad-ul-Ibad* of Najmuddin Razi (died 1123), *Maktubat* of Ain-ul-Quzat (died 1131), *Lawaih* and *Lawami* of Qazi Hamiduddin Nagauri and our most famous text, *Fawa'id-ul-Fu'ad*, the spiritual sayings of Hazrat Nizamuddin, compiled by Amir Hasan Sijzi.[24]

Thus, the period witnessed the rise of Hazrat Nizamuddin in the same mould as the earliest of the Sufi masters, such as Shaikh Junaid Baghdadi (died 910) and Shaikh Bayazid Bustami (died 875). According to Barani, God adorned Hazrat Nizamuddin with His own love in a way that would be difficult to comprehend by human intellect, as if the accomplishments and attributes of sainthood were bestowed upon him in their best and final shape, and the art of guiding people to the right path was brought to an end. Like Amir Hasan earlier,

Barani also declared Hazrat Nizamuddin as the seal of the saints:

> Do not seek renown in this art
> It had attained its culmination in the person of Nizami.[25]

14

THE GLORIOUS CHISHTI TRADITION

> The spiritual genealogy of the Chishti Sufis (*khwajagan*) goes back to Prophet Muhammad through Amir-ul-Muminin Hazrat Ali down to Sultan-ul-Mashaikh Hazrat Khwaja Nizamuddin Auliya; and Khwaja Muinuddin Chishti, the keeper of divine secrets, was the deputy of the Prophet of Islam on the land of Hindustan.
>
> – *Siyar-ul-Auliya* of Amir Khwurd Kirmani

The glorious Chishti Sufi tradition in India, which has long been respected for centuries, began with the phenomenal career of the founder of the order, Sultan-ul-Hind Khwaja

Gharib Nawaz Muinuddin Chishti of Ajmer (1143–1236). Born in Sistan in eastern Iran, Muinuddin relocated to India at the time of the establishment of the Delhi Sultanate in the late twelfth century and worked with his equally distinguished disciple and successor Khwaja Qutbuddin Bakhtiyar Kaki (1173–1235), who was settled in Delhi and after whom Delhi's architectural marvel, the Qutub Minar, was named. Bakhtiyar Kaki's enigmatic and illustrious successor, Khwaja Fariduddin Ganj-i-Shakar, popularly known as Shaikh Farid and Baba Farid (1173–1265), shaped for centuries to come both the character of Islam in the region of Punjab and its vibrant and eclectic cultural traditions generally. The saint was clairvoyant in noticing the excellence of the young Hazrat Nizamuddin, who was to carry forward and strengthen the foundations of the Chishti tradition with his towering presence in Delhi in decades to come and a lasting legacy across regions and centuries. Khwaja Nasiruddin Chiragh-i-Dehli (1274–1356) was his most devoted follower who abandoned a comfortable life as a member of a merchant family in Awadh to endure excruciating pain as an ascetic completely devoted to the love of God. Chiragh-i-Dehli completed the superlative chain of Sufis who flourished in India in the thirteenth and fourteenth centuries.

Many disciples and successors of these early Sufi masters spread across the subcontinent to disseminate their life's work. This significantly influenced India's development into a pluralistic culture where remarkable diversity coexisted with mutual respect. Through their practice, the Chishti Sufis were able to show a tolerant face of Muslim society, which now tends to get sidelined in times of violent assertions of political Islam. As shown in previous chapters, some of the important themes and issues common to Sufi traditions include contested practices such as *karamat* or miracles, musical assemblies, *qawwali* and other forms of poetry of love, and relations with custodians of Sunni Islam as well as ruling regimes, especially the sultans of Delhi, with whom there was a conflict of claims to authority. Together, all these add to the formation of a lasting tradition of cultural achievements, communal harmony and spiritually soaked environment at Sufi shrines, called *dargahs*. Purification of the soul, cultivation of the heart which is completely devoted in its love for God and – since He is supposed to be the creator of everything – love and respect for all His creations are also important features of Sufism. In this chapter, some of these features of considerable import will be discussed with reference to brief accounts, following the old *tazkira* or biography style, from the lives of Hazrat Nizamuddin's predecessors as well as the successor in the Chishti spiritual lineage (*silsila*). Together they formed a glorious tradition of Chishti Sufis, deeply venerated across the Indian subcontinent and beyond for centuries to come.

Khwaja Gharib Nawaz Muinuddin Chishti of Ajmer

> God keeps as friends the people with following three characteristics: first, generosity like the sea; second, affection like sun; and three, modesty and hospitality like the earth.
>
> – Muinuddin Chishti's teaching as recorded in the mid-fourteenth century Sufi biographical text, *Siyar-ul-Auliya* of Amir Khwurd Kirmani.[1]

For Khwaja Muinuddin Chishti, the cultivation of a human soul with attributes like those of the sea, the sun and the earth, which do not discriminate with people in sharing their fine natural resources, can make people fine human beings who will be considered friends of God. For such blessed people, the best prayers in the eyes of the beloved God comprised looking after the concerns of the impoverished people, providing for the needs of the poor and offering food to the hungry.[2] Respect for God's creation is one aspect of the recommended moral conduct and veneration of God is another. No amount of devotion to God is enough for salvation, if His creation is hurt or harmed by the person concerned. Therefore, as mentioned previously, there are two aspects in the teachings of the Chishti tradition emphasized early by Khwaja Muinuddin Chishti: a human being's relation with other human beings and their relation with God. Excellence in both is the recommended way of life.

As the saints never die, a life devoted to the love of God and service to humanity will have a lasting significance. Millions of visitors to Muinuddin Chishti's *dargah* and the ritual Sufic *chaadar* regularly sent by even people in power testify to the continuing belief in the powers of blessings and benediction surrounding the khwaja's *mazar*. This is despite the fact that the saint himself liked to maintain distance from people, especially those in power. Avoiding people in power, the reigning sultans of Delhi, was a particularly cherished practice in the Chishti tradition. The people in power, on the other hand, always attempted to partake in the blessings accrued from their association with the Chishti saints and their *daraghs*. The Sufi position about maintaining distance from people in power meant the ideals of separating religion and spirituality from the practices of the state, something of the kind identified as secularism in modern times. In this understanding, religion can be the private aspects of the practitioners and politics and government deal with the public life of the people. Those in power have not generally respected this distinction that the Sufis wanted to ensure in their lives at least. At the same time, Sufis were also not expected to maintain complete aloofness from political developments affecting the lives of the people. They were not expected to lead a withdrawn and ascetic life devoted to meditation in seclusion. They had to live amongst the people and endure the difficulties of the time. Large crowds will always be thronging around them for help and guidance, spiritual and material. Considered to be close to God, they were expected to set things right.

Besides *Siyar-ul-Auliya*, quoted above, details of the life and teachings of Muinuddin Chishti are also available in collections of discourses attributed to him and Qutbuddin Bakhtiyar Kaki from a very early period. These include *Dalil-ul-'Arifin* (Soulful Conversations of Muinuddin Chishti Collected by Qutbuddin Bakhtiyar Kaki) and *Fawa'id-us-Salikin* (Spiritual Utterances of Qutbuddin Bakhtiyar Kaki compiled by Baba Farid).[3] Besides *Asrar-ul-Auliya,* the collection of the *malfuzat* of Fariduddin Ganj-i-Shakar also contained several anecdotes related to the shaikh.[4] Hazrat Nizamuddin also referred to Khwaja Muinuddin Chishti with a lot of respect, for instance, in one case in which Khwaja Wahiduddin, a grandson of Muinuddin Chishti, came to Baba Farid and requested to accept him as a disciple. The latter told him that he was blessed with the chain of spirituality introduced by his own grandfather, but Wahiduddin insisted on becoming a disciple; he took Baba Farid's hand, expressing an oath of allegiance as a disciple (*murid*) and also got himself tonsured as a mark of joining the mystic path.[5]

The near-contemporary texts portray Khwaja Muinuddin Chishti being trained in Islamic mysticism by his *pir*, Khwaja Usman Harwani;[6] travelling with him to distant Islamic lands; expressing his concern over the indifference of the Muslims towards prayers; narrating the accounts of miracles performed by his *pir* and also by himself.[7] The shaikh is also shown spiritually transported to visit the *Ka'ba* every night, and when the shaikh stopped doing so, the latter came to circumambulate him.[8] The image of the shaikh that emerged in the mind of the reader of these texts was one of a preacher and Islamizer with considerable charismatic power. Amir Khwurd standardized this image in his *Siyar-ul-Auliya.* He wrote that infidelity and idol worship were widespread in the whole of Hindustan before the arrival of the shaikh. The people worshipped stones, trees and animals. Their hearts were sealed in the darkness of infidelity. With the arrival of the shaikh, the dark clouds of ignorance gave way to the spiritual light of Islam.[9]

Amir Khwurd also wrote quoting Nizamuddin Auliya that when Muinuddin Chishti reached Ajmer, Rai Pithaura (Prithviraj Chauhan) was ruling from there. Rai Pithaura and his high officials resented the shaikh's presence in their city. However, the latter's eminence and his apparent power to perform miracles prompted them to refrain from taking action against him. A disciple of the shaikh who was in the service of Rai Pithaura began to receive a hostile treatment from the king. The shaikh sent a message on his behalf. Rai Pithaura refused to accept the recommendation, indicating his resentment of the shaikh's alleged claims to understand the secrets of the Unseen. When the shaikh (referred to as *badshah-i-islam*) heard this, he prophesied: 'We have seized Pithaura alive and handed him over to the army of Islam' (*Pithaura ra zinde giraftim wa dadim be-lashkar-i-islam*). About the same time, Muizuddin Sam's army arrived from Ghaznin and defeated him.[10] Muinuddin's charismatic presence in Hindustan at the time of the emergence of the Delhi Sultanate in the late twelfth century makes him, for followers, a true Sultan-ul-Hind. In posterity, where he had settled and where his *dargah* is located, is considered by his devout followers as something of the Mecca of Islam in India – a major pilgrimage site spreading the message of love and peace in society.

Khwaja Muinuddin taught his disciples that the company of noble people is better than any act of kindness, and the company of bad people is worse than any act of sinning. A life completely free of sins is not possible, but continuous prayers for repentance can ensure that the angels stationed on one's left side do not register any sins committed for twenty years. A life with a burning heart in love with God picks up the attributes of God.[11] At the time of Muinuddin's passing away, his forehead was inscribed with the following statement: *habib allah maat fi hubb allah* (a friend of God left the world in love of God).[12] Much revered in later devotional traditions, his spiritual presence and blessings were powerfully invoked by Mughal princess Jahanara Begam in the middle of the seventeenth century in her *Munis-ul-Arwah*, through the following couplet, which sums up the essence of Sufism and veneration of Sufi saints in posterity:[13]

Muinuddin-i ma fanist dar haq
Az aan baqi shudan dar zat-i mutlaq

Our Muinuddin is annihilated in God
From that he subsists in the absolute essence.[14]

Khwaja Qutbuddin Bakhtiyar Kaki

There are significant connections between the emergence of Delhi as a major Sufi centre and sanctuary of Islam as well as a strong seat of political power, known for its cosmopolitan cultural excellence. Three out of the first five 'great' Chishtis of the Sultanate period chose to live in Delhi, and their tombs have subsequently contributed to the process of sacralization of the place, appropriating it as a Chishti *wilayat* and, indeed, providing it the respectable sobriquet of 'Hazrat-i-Dehli', or venerable Delhi. The city acquired the status of the foremost centre of Islam at a time when the Mongol upsurge had led to the destruction of major Islamic cities in Central Asia, Iran and the Middle East, including Samarkand, Bukhara and Baghdad. Indeed, Delhi served as a refuge to a host of displaced immigrant populations who brought with them a variety of religious and intellectual traditions, leading to contestations amongst various claimants to power and authority. Yet, to start with, it was the liberal and accommodative Chishtis who endowed it with a cosmopolitan character, preventing it from taking a homogeneous shape. The institutionalized and devout (*ba-sha'ra*) Chishtis distanced themselves from, and even opposed, the extremist agenda of giving the option of Islam or death to non-Muslims, yet they ensured that the interests of Islam and Muslims were safeguarded. Though the urban conglomerate of Delhi remained the bastion of Muslim power for close to six centuries and its landscape is dotted with mosques, *madrasas* (Islamic seminaries) and *dargahs* of Sufis, the exclusionist, juridical interpretation of *shari'at* was set aside in favour of a more inclusive approach to Islam practised and propagated by the Chishti Sufis. This accommodative character of religious practices in the capital city also shaped the pluralistic and broad-based polity of the country.

Muinuddin Chishti had chosen a sophisticated and accomplished Sufi Khwaja Qutbuddin Bakhtiyar Kaki for the cosmopolitan *wilayat* of Delhi. Bakhtiyar Kaki was born at Ush, located on the bank of the river Jaxartes in Central Asia. He had met Muinuddin for the first time while staying in Baghdad and had become his disciple. Bakhtiyar Kaki followed his *pir,* Muinuddin, and reached Delhi in the reign of Shamsuddin Iltutmish. The sultan welcomed the shaikh and invited him to live in the city. Hesitant at first, he agreed to the ruler's request. Bakhtiyar Kaki, called so for his supposedly miraculous ability to produce *kak,* or bread, to sustain his family, had to compete for space in the spiritual geography of the city. Not to talk of the *ulama,* quite a few eminent Sufi shaikhs of various orders had come to settle there. Many of them had just arrived following Mongol invasions in Central Asia and Iran. Bakhtiyar Kaki found the most powerful antagonist in Shaikhul Islam Najmuddin Sughra, a Sufi of his own order. Najmuddin and Bakhtiyar Kaki's *pir* Muinuddin were disciples of the same shaikh, Khwaja Usman Harwani. Najmuddin was not taking kindly to the growing popularity of Bakhtiyar Kaki and his influence in the political circles of Delhi. Iltutmish himself was a devotee, and, according to a later tradition, had become a *khalifa* or spiritual successor of the shaikh.

Seeking to prevent the tension between Najmuddin and Bakhtiyar Kaki from escalating, Muinuddin, who was on a visit to Delhi, asked his disciple to leave the place and accompany him to Ajmer. The news of the departure of the saints was perceived as a sign of calamity by the sultan and the people. They followed the shaikhs for miles – crying and wailing. Touched by the grief of the ruler and the ruled alike, Muinuddin allowed Bakhtiyar Kaki to remain in Delhi. As a patron saint of the city, Kaki enjoyed prestige and authority and influenced the sultan's style of governance. It is related that once the Prophet appeared in dreams to both the Sufi and the sultan and indicated a particular spot for building a tank (Hauz-i-Shamsi) to overcome Delhi's water shortage.

The site of Hauz-i-Shamsi, along with the adjacent Auliya Masjid, Jahaz Mahal and the Jharna (a picturesque spring garden), was significant not only as a source of water but also became a rendezvous of the spiritual and intellectual elite of the city. Much to the chagrin of puritanical *ulama*, music assemblies (*mahfil-i-sama, qawwali*) were frequently organized, Chishti Sufi Bakhtiyar Kaki being the moving spirit behind them. As later informed by Hazrat Nizamuddin, speaking to his disciples, the shaikh died in an ecstatic state induced by mystical poetry recited in a *sama*, listening to a particular couplet for over four days:

Kushtagan-i khanjar-i taslim ra,
Har zaman as ghayb jani-i digar ast

To the victims of the dagger of submission,
There comes a new life from the unseen every moment.[15]

His funeral prayer (*namaz-i-janaza*) was to be led by the most pious person in the dominion. It was none other than Sultan Shamsuddin Iltutmish, celebrated in Sufi tradition as a mystic in the garb of a king. The saint was buried in Mehrauli at a lonely place he himself had chosen. The burial of several Sufis and rulers in the vicinity led to the emergence of a big necropolis over the centuries. The shrine complex and its neighbourhood had become very crowded by early fourteenth century as recorded in *Fawa'id-ul-Fu'ad, malfuzat* of Hazrat Nizamuddin Auliya. Iltutmish survived the shaikh for only a few months and was interned in an elegant tomb of his own in Qutub complex, not far from Bakhtiyar Kaki's *dargah*. Knowingly or otherwise, the sultan, whose authority as head of hierarchy of theologians and jurists was undisputed, followed his contemporary Abbasid caliph, al-Nasir's, approach of using prominent Sufi order as official organization of popular Islam under the ruler, combining pietistic legality of the *ulama* with spiritual adventures of Chishti Sufis. No wonder, Sufi institutions like *khanaqahs* and *jama'at-khanas* flourished along with mosques and *madrasas*.

Shaikh Fariduddin Ganj-i-Shakar

> Today, I have planted a tree whose shade will provide comfort to many creations of God.
>
> – Baba Farid on appointing Nizamuddin a disciple and successor in Chishti Sufism[16]

Khwaja Qutbuddin Bakhtiyar Kaki's successor in the Chishti order of Sufis and Hazrat Nizamuddin's preceptor, Shaikh Fariduddin Ganj-i-Shakar (Shaikh Farid or Baba Farid) was born in a respected Muslim family at Kahtawal, a town near Multan, sometime in 1175. He was sent to a school (*madrasa*) where he memorized the Qur'an and went on to specialize in Arabic grammar, Qura'nic commentaries (*tafsir*) and Islamic jurisprudence (*fiqh*), before reportedly travelling to the major centres of Islamic learning in West Asia.[17] The erudite young scholar Shaikh Farid had met Bakhtiyar Kaki at Multan and joined the Chishti order as a disciple. Before his death, Bakhtiyar Kaki had nominated Shaikh Farid as his spiritual successor. Farid was at Hansi, in Hisar district (in Haryana), at the time and could only reach Delhi three days later. Soon, the shaikh decided to leave for Hansi, despite reminders from the fellow mystics and followers that Bakhtiyar Kaki had chosen him for the *wilayat* of Delhi. Shaikh Farid defended his decision to go; he was sunk so deep in devotion that he could no longer differentiate between a city and a desert. He may have been uncomfortable with Delhi's aggressive political machinations. Bakhtiyar Kaki's troubles with his fellow shaikhs in the city may also have been at the back of his mind. Shaikh Farid thus returned to Hansi, before permanently shifting to Ajodhan, deferentially referred to as Pakpattan, now in Punjab, Pakistan. It is at Ajodhan that Farid's reputation as a charismatic spiritual leader was built, which made him a living legend and one of Punjab's all-time great Sufi saints in centuries to come.[18]

Hazrat Nizamuddin frequently referred to the extraordinary qualities of his spiritual master, Shaikh Farid, some of which were recorded by Amir Hasan Sijzi in *Fawa'id-ul-Fu'ad*. Nizamuddin also collected Farid's teachings, and a collection of spiritual conversations (*malfuzat*) of the saint (*farid*) compiled by the disciple (Nizamuddin), *Rahat-ul-Qulub*, is available in Sufi circles since around the middle of the fourteenth century. Farid's discourses were also compiled in a volume, *Asrar-ul-Auliya*, by his disciple and son-in-law, Shaikh Bahauddin Ishaq. Besides, Shaikh Farid himself is known in posterity for collecting the teachings of his preceptor Bakhtiyar Kaki in a volume titled, *Fawa'id-us-Salikin*. Amir Khwurd's authoritative collection of Chishti Sufi biographies, *Siyar-ul-Auliya*, brings together much of the information available in these texts. Later writers added their own information from written texts and oral traditions to build the narrative further. Of these, Shaikh Jamali's *Siyar-ul-Arifin* (early sixteenth century) and Shaikh Abdul Haq Muhaddis Dehlawi's *Akhbar-ul-Akhyar* (late sixteenth century) present interesting dimensions of Shaikh Farid's personality as a Sufi saint – rooted in Islam's grand tradition even as he appropriated and adapted mystical ideas and exercises from diverse sources.

Shaikh Farid's charisma is traced back to his childhood, as early as his birth. It is suggested that there was some confusion concerning the beginning of Ramazan, as the moon was not sighted at the place – an ongoing problem for Muslims in the Indian subcontinent. A saintly person visiting Farid's father, Jamaluddin Sulaiman, said that if the latter's infant son took milk in the morning, it might be assumed that the fast of Ramazan had not begun. As it turned out, the baby did not feed the whole day, which signified that the fast had started. Meanwhile, news came from far and near, supported by a religious announcement (*fatwa*) from Multan that Ramazan had indeed started. The child continued his 'fast' for the whole month, as he would take milk only after sunset.[19] Growing up as a mystically inclined, precocious young boy, Farid was already known in the territory around Punjab as a *diwana bachcha* (mad child).[20]

In years to come, extreme hunger due to fasting for days would earn him the title of Ganj-i-Shakar (a storehouse of sugar). It is related by Amir Khwurd that some pebbles, which he had put in his mouth during fasting for three consecutive days, had turned into sugar with the blessings of God. In the early sixteenth century, Shaikh Jamali recorded that one day, Shaikh Farid was going to see his preceptor, Bakhtiyar Kaki. He was wearing wooden sandals and the roads were muddy because of the rain. Weak due to fasting for seven days at a stretch, Farid fell. Some mud went inside his mouth and immediately turned into sugar. Later, Abdul Haq added another interesting story. A merchant had come to meet the shaikh at Ajodhan. He was carrying sugar with him, and lied, saying it was salt. Unhappy, the shaikh remarked that it must actually be salt. Later, on opening the sacks, the merchant found to his dismay that the sugar had been converted into salt. He rushed to the shaikh and begged for forgiveness. The shaikh's prayers transformed the salt back into sugar. From that time, he came to be known as Ganj-i-Shakar. Not satisfied with such tales, later reporters came up with their own versions, which sent the origin of the title backwards in time once again to his childhood. It is suggested that as a child, Farid was fond of sugar. His mother had told him that God sent sugar to the boys who punctually offered their morning prayers and kept some sugar under his pillow every night. When Farid reached his twelfth year, his mother stopped putting the packet of sugar. It was, however, discovered that the divine 'gift' continued to reach him.[21]

Such extraordinary stories abound in Sufi literature about the power and charisma attributed to Shaikh Farid from very early in his life. Such a reputation also meant that he was widely popular amongst both the poor and the rich. The powerful Turkish noble, Ulugh Khan, who went on to be the most despotic of Delhi sultans, Ghiyasuddin Balban, offered his daughter in marriage to Shaikh Farid, with whom he had several children. Farid maintained critical distance from the sultan, and instead of enjoying benefits from his royal connections to live a comfortable life, he preferred a life in poverty. The most important thing he did for our purpose here and for the Chishti tradition was to quickly realize that the future saint Hazrat Nizamuddin was the person who would carry forward the tradition from his base in Delhi. Nizamuddin had moved from Badaun to Delhi and was looking for a government job, such as that of a *qazi*. A serendipitous meeting with Shaikh Farid's brother, Najibuddin Mutawakkil, in Delhi changed Nizamuddin's life forever. Mutawakkil advised him not to become a *qazi* but be something else instead. Mutawakkil promptly took Nizamuddin to meet Shaikh Farid in Punjab, where he became a disciple of the saint poet, whose verses he had heard as a child from faqirs and dervishes singing in Badaun. Trained in the mystic path by one of the fine souls around, Nizamuddin remembered and referred frequently to his spiritual master for the rest of his life as the great saint (Shaikh Kabir).

It is related that when a fellow student, in older times, saw Nizamuddin in a shabby condition in old and worn-out clothes after joining the mystic path, he questioned the wisdom of deliberately choosing a life of poverty and suggested that Nizamuddin could have a led a dignified life as a teacher, as the income from that could have taken care of his creature comforts. Spiritually informed of Nizamuddin being accosted, Shaikh Farid miraculously arranged to send a platter of fine food for that old friend of the former. The embarrassed friend was also told through this couplet:

Na hamrahi tu mara rah-i-khwish gir-o bor-o
Tura sa'adat bada mara nigun-sari

You are not a companion, go and take your own path
Enjoy your good fortune, I am fine in my modesty.[22]

Witness to both the miracle and candidness in the poetry above, the antagonist rushed to become a disciple of Shaikh Farid. His hospice and later his tomb also attracted the local population in large numbers. The shaikh recommended recitation of prayers in local dialects and thus contributed to the growth of vernacular, mainly Urdu and Punjabi, languages. A large number of verses attributed to Shaikh Farid were included by the Sikh Gurus in the Adi Granth. Though some scholars have suggested that Shaikh Farid was not the actual author of the verses incorporated in the *Farid-bani,* their inclusion by the Gurus in their 'book' demonstrate the universal appeal of the Sufi saints in medieval India. Shaikh Farid's teachings not only helped in the widening of the Chishti order but also in the propagation of Islam in the region of Punjab. His disciples played an important role in the dissemination of his teachings far and wide. Hazrat Nizamuddin played the most important role in this process of shaping and strengthening the Chishti tradition in large parts of the Indian subcontinent.[23]

Shaikh Nasiruddin Mahmud Chiragh-i-Dehli

Miyan-i jumla-i ashaab hamchu mahi bood
Che nisbat bood be-mah balke badshahe bood

Amongst all the fellow companions he was like a moon
Even moon was not comparable, he was like a king (among the Sufis).

– Amir Khwurd Kirmani in his *Siyar-ul-Auliya*[24]

Hazrat Nizamuddin Auliya had selected Nasiruddin Chiragh-i-Dehli to lead the Chishti order in the next generation. Of a large number of disciples, companions, friends and spiritual successors of Nizamuddin Auliya, Nasiruddin turned out to be the most appropriate mystic to form part of the grand cycle of the first five Chishti Sufis in all their excellence as spiritual figures who fit the expectations of what it meant to be a great Chishti master, Khwaja. After Nizamuddin's passing away, Nasiruddin conducted himself amidst the large numbers of the former's disciples in such a way that they felt that the tradition strengthened by Nizamuddin had continued to function without any disruption. Amir Khwurd, a fellow mystic, poet and

Sufi biographer, writes that Nasiruddin was much rewarded with spiritual benefits and training in the mystic path by Nizamuddin Auliya in his lifetime and has continued to excel with his conduct in decades to come, not departing from the Chishti tradition in any way.[25]

Shaikh Nasiruddin was born in Awadh (Ayodhya). His father, a textile merchant, died when the shaikh was still a young boy. He received an education in traditional Islamic learning before giving up on the family business to devote his time to prayers and meditation. Moving to Delhi in his early forties, he used his close friendship with Amir Khusrau to become a disciple of Nizamuddin Auliya, and eventually a close companion and leading successor in the Chishti *silsila*. That he was an educated man from a well-to-do Syed family (descendant of the Prophet) and had abandoned this worldly comfort to become completely devoted to Sufism mattered to Nizamuddin as a prospect for the candidate who would carry forward the Chishti tradition. Like the authoritative collection of discourses of Nizamuddin Auliya, *Fawa'id-ul-Fu'ad*, Nasiruddin's discourses were collected by Hamid Qalandar, a poet and disciple, in a compilation called *Khair-ul-Majalis*. Amir Khwurd Kirmani and later Abdul

Haq Muhaddis Dehlawi used this text to highlight the fine qualities in their biographies of Nasiruddin Chiragh as an accomplished Chishti Sufi saint.[26]

Hazrat Nizamuddin had told Nasiruddin that renunciation did not mean that he was going to live in a jungle to lead the life of an ascetic; instead, he was expected to stay with the people and endure their demands of different kinds. Most oppressive demand, bordering on torture, came from the despotic ruler, Sultan Muhammad Tughlaq. The sultan had acquired power with the reported blessings of Hazrat Nizamuddin, but he turned against the Sufis no sooner than he had captured power after a ghastly removal of his father, Sultan Ghiyasuddin (who had harassed Nizamuddin as we have seen above). Muhammad Tughlaq, in turn, began to harass Nizamuddin's disciples, forcing some to migrate to Daulatabad and others who refused to migrate, as did Nasiruddin, to serve him in his court and palace, reducing him to the status of a veritable personal servant. Folk memory celebrates Nasiruddin's resistance to the dictates of the sultan, giving him the title of Chiragh, for his was considered to be the only house in Delhi where the lamp kept burning at night at the time when migration to Delhi was forcibly attempted by the sultan.

A despot, Muhammad Tughlaq, ruled large parts of the subcontinent but remained insecure in his power for the majority of his rule. The humiliation he heaped on the Chishtis was considered particularly unacceptable in the Sufi fraternities. When people asked Shaikh Nasiruddin why he continued to silently endure the absurd violations, Nasiruddin replied in the typically Sufi idiom that the matter was between him and God, and the latter puts his loving creatures under a lot of difficulties to test their enduring capacity.[27] In an anecdote recorded in *Akhbar-ul-Akhyar* of Abdul Haq Muhaddis Dehlawi, it is mentioned that Muhammad Tughlaq once sent to Shaikh Nasiruddin some food in utensils of gold and silver. His intention was to question the shaikh on refusing to consume food as rejection and disrespect, and in case he accepted and ate the food, he could be interrogated for eating food in utensils made of precious metals, which was not approved in certain interpretations of Islam. When the food was brought before the shaikh, he took some gravy from one of the utensils made of gold, put it in his palm, and tasted it. He was, thus, able to evade the evil design of the wicked sultan to corner and harass him on Islamic legal grounds.[28]

Eventually, Amir Khwurd writes with some

satisfaction that when the sultan died during his last campaign at Thatha in Sindh, harassing Nasiruddin and other Sufis all along, he was eventually brought down from the mighty throne of the Sultanate and his mortal remains were brought to Delhi in a wooden coffin (*badshah mazkur ra az takht-i saltanat dar takhta-i taabut kardeh dar shahr award*).[29] Thus, as is famously known, both the despotic ruler and the hapless public got rid of each other. Hazrat Nizamuddin had already warned Muhammad Tughlaq's father and predecessor, Sultan Ghiyasuddin, not to harass the Sufis for his own good: *hunuz dilli dur ast*! People in power think they will be in power forever and not be accountable for all their violations. On the other hand, those suffering must show an extraordinary capacity for endurance. Suppressed people survive to write their own histories.

Commenting on complete dependence on the will of God on the part of the Sufis, blessed disciples of Hazrat Nizamuddin, Amir Khwurd further wrote:

Sher nar bosad be-hurmat mard-e qaane ra qadam
Pir sag khayad be-dandaan paye mard-e har dare

A male lion reverentially kisses the feet of the content man
And an old dog bites the leg of a man who begs from door to door.[30]

In conclusion, uncomfortable with the materialistic attitudes of the time, the widespread political unrest, theologians' continual questioning of music-induced ecstasy and people's expectation of all kinds of miracles to be performed by the Sufis – as in the case of demanding prayers for rain – Nasiruddin Chiragh increasingly distanced himself from these demands. He remarked that people treated mysticism as a child's play, rather than a life bound by law. He urged, quoting Persian poet, Shaikh Sanai of Ghazna:

Musalmanan Musalmanan musalmani musalmani
Az-in ayin-i be-dinaan pashimani pashimani

Muslims must follow the path of musalmani, as a faithful believer
This practice of the faithless is a matter of shame, repent, repent.[31]

15

CONCLUSION: EXTRAORDINARY LOVER OF GOD

Aan ruz keh mah shudi na-mi-daanisti
Ka-angusht numaaye alami khwahi shud
Imruz keh zulfat dil-i khalqi barbood
Dar goshe nashistanat na-mi-daarad sood

When you appeared on the day like a moon, did you not know that fingers will be raised around the world?
Now that the hearts of people are enchanted by the locks of your hair, there is no point in going away to sit in hiding.

– As quoted in *Fawa'id-ul-Fu'ad*

As mentioned previously, disturbed by the large crowds of people thronging his hospice at Ghiyaspur, not far from where he is buried now, Hazrat Nizamuddin was contemplating moving to a lonelier place where he could spend his time in complete devotion to God. This was pre-empted by a handsome young visitor, who was never seen before or after, who recited the above couplet and advised Hazrat Nizamuddin not to leave the place, saying that he should not have become famous in the first place, but since it was so, he could not now run away from the great expectations people have from him. This would not be appreciated by the Prophet of Islam, Muhammad, and facing him on the day of judgement would be difficult. According to the saint, the young man said enduring the demands of people and patiently serving them was part of devotion and prayers to God.[1]

Summing up the fascinating details of the enthralling characteristics of Hazrat Nizamuddin Auliya and his circle of the formidable Chishti Sufi masters and huge numbers of devoted followers, it is evident that this spiritual movement is renowned across history in the Indian subcontinent and beyond. This movement has been dedicated to the love of God and respect for all his creations. Sufism has historically spread to all parts of the known world. Wherever the Sufis went, they got themselves embedded in local customs and practices. They played important social and cultural roles in shaping and transforming the society with their message of universal brotherhood, egalitarianism, tolerance and respect for difference. This is what we have seen in much detail in the foregoing pages, from the life of Hazrat Nizamuddin and other charismatic Sufi masters of the glorious medieval Chishti tradition. Later custodians of this tradition have continued to show that the shrines and tombs (*mazars* and *dargahs*) of Sufis remain relevant in modern times. A large majority of Muslims in India follow peace-loving Sufi-oriented Islam, and at the same time, a large majority of visitors to Sufi shrines are non-Muslims! It is about transcending the politically controlled religious boundary markers, which the Sufis also defied.

There is a vast corpus of Sufi literature in a variety of languages, forms and genres. These voluminous Sufi writings help in understanding the critical social, cultural and political roles Sufis have performed historically. The Sufi masters, such as Hazrat Nizamuddin and his other Sufi associates, insisted on ethical concerns, for making themselves and their followers acceptable in the eyes of the merciful and loving God. These Sufis considered themselves friends and lovers of God and strove to cultivate awe-inspiring credentials. The main features were love for the eternal divine and respect for all his creations, whether humans or non-humans and irrespective of caste, creed or gender. All these called for some compassion and some broad humanism. The discourses of Hazrat Nizamuddin, admired in Sufi tradition not merely as a lover of God but also a beloved of God, reveal a continuous reiteration of ethical precepts important for general human conduct. Nizamuddin's spiritually imbued conversations (*malfuzat*), *Fawa'id-ul-Fu'ad*, is a superlative guide on how to become a good human being despite all the ugliness of the world pulling people down.

As we have seen, the institutions of Sufis have long been open for women to seek blessings and benediction. Despite patriarchal restrictions in society, some women themselves have gone on to distinguish themselves with charisma and power, which they used for the benefit of the people. The medieval Indian Sufi literature has long referred to women in respectful terms. The literature includes anecdotes related to saintly women, making them recognized in both popular perception and in Sufi fraternities as evolved and blessed souls in their own right. Examples of episodes from the lives of some such charismatic personalities from medieval India illustrate how they were valued in their own times and celebrated as well as invoked in posterity. Hazrat Nizamuddin frequently remembered several graceful and charismatic women he had known or heard about, including his own saintly mother, Bibi Zulaikha, and an illustrious woman among the Sufis, Fatima Sam of Delhi. The shrines of some of these women mystics remain important for centuries after their death. Sufi tradition believes that saints never die. They continue to function for the general public's well-being even while resting in their graves. Thus, their tombs attract large numbers of people, especially on Thursday nights and on the occasion of their death anniversary. Once again, central to all these are love for God and love and respect for all His creations.

Among many rituals and practices, devotional movements are historically known for their singing songs of love for the divine. Sufi music is also about love for God and care for all his creations. Struggles over Sufi music and dance have a long history, with artists and connoisseurs running into difficulties with the custodians of public morality backed by political regimes. Yet for all their powers, they have not been able to suppress the artists and art forms forever. Hazrat Nizamuddin endured serious troubles on account of his interest in *qawwali*. Though there were other political issues behind the harassment, Nizamuddin Auliya was forced to attend a judicial interrogation (*mahzar*) at Sultan Ghiyasuddin Tughlaq's court. He was asked to defend his interest in Sufi music (*sama* and *qawwali*) in the light of the prevalent *shari'at*. His arguments more or less settled the issue of the legitimacy of Sufi music as a popular and devotional art form, despite occasional attacks from irrational fanatics, who occasionally seek to suppress Sufi practices in all their varied spiritual dimensions.

As Hazrat Nizamuddin continuously emphasized, Sufism advocates for the peaceful coexistence of all the wide diversity of people. This is especially important in troubled political times when narrowly defined religious boundaries and aggressive politics of religion are creating a serious humanitarian crisis. Politicians and other interested parties who thrive on violence are creating faultlines between communities of people and pitting them against one another in the name of religion and community. The Sufi message of peace with all offers an alternative for hope. *Sajjadanashins* and spiritual leaders associated with Sufi shrines are keeping the traditions of Sufi teachings alive. They have kept the gates of *dargahs* open to all visitors and followers, including women, non-Muslims, poor and others, who also seek blessings and benediction, offering flowers and ritual Sufic *chaadars*, especially on celebrations. The Sufis are believed to achieve union with their beloved God once they have passed away. As the saints never die, their spiritual blessings continue to benefit the devotees. On their part, Sufis were always concerned about the day of judgement and life after death; how would God treat them? During one of his conversations, Hazrat Nizamuddin had mentioned how a leading thirteenth-century Sufi saint, Shaikh Saifuddin Bakharzi, had publicly announced his own passing away as a painful detachment from the world, which was not an easy proposition, despite spending a lifetime of seeking union with God:

Raftam aye yaraan ba-samaan khair baad
Neest aasaan dard-i hijraan khair baad

Friends, I am leaving, goodbye to this material world
The pain of separation is hurting, goodbye nonetheless! [2]

NOTES

1. Introduction: Beloved of God

1. Amir Hasan Sijzi, *Fawa'id-ul-Fu'ad*, conversations of Shaikh Nizamuddin Auliya (Delhi: Urdu Academy, 1990). For the Persian couplet, see Ibid., p. 36. For the earliest hagiographical account of Hazrat Nizamuddin's life, see Muhammad Jamal Qiwam, *Qiwam-ul-'Aqa'id* (Rampur, U.P.: Nashr-o-Isha'at, 1994). Also see Amir Khwurd Kirmani, *Siyar-ul-Auliya* (Islamabad: Markaz Tahqiqat-i-Farsi Iran wa Pakistan, 1978) and Shaikh Abdul Haq Muhaddis Dehlawi, *Akhbar-ul-Akhyar*, ed. Alim Ashraf Khan (Tehran: Society for the Appreciation of Cultural Works and Dignitaries, 2005). For a modern biography, see K. A. Nizami, *Life and Times of Shaikh Nizamuddin Auliya* (New Delhi: Idarah-i Adabiyat-i Delli, 1991).
2. Mohammad Habib, *Politics and Society during the Early Medieval Period, Collected Works* vol. 1, ed. K. A. Nizami (New Delhi: People's Publishing House,

1974); S. Nurul Hasan, *Religion, State, and Society in Medieval India* (New Delhi: Oxford University Press, 2005); K. A. Nizami, *Some Aspects of Religion and Politics in India* (Aligarh: Department of History, 1961); Saiyid Athar Abbas Rizvi, *A History of Sufism in India* vol. I (New Delhi: Munshiram Manoharlal, 1978); Carl W. Ernst, *Eternal Garden: Mysticism, History, and Politics at a South Asian Sufi Center* (New York: State University of New York Press, 1992). Also see Bruce B. Lawrence, *Notes from a Distant Flute: The Extant Literature of pre-Mughal Indian Sufism* (Tehran: Imperial Iranian Academy of Philosophy, 1978); Carl W. Ernst and Bruce B. Lawrence, *Sufi Martyrs of Love: The Chishti Order in South Asia and Beyond* (New York: Palgrave Macmillan, 2002).

3. Simon Digby, 'The Sufi Shaykh As a Source of Authority in Medieval India', *Purushartha* vol. 9, pp. 55–77; 'Qalandars and Related Groups' in Yohanan Friedman, *Islam in Asia*, vol. 1, pp. 67–8 (1984); Richard M. Eaton, *Sufis of Bijapur* and *Essays on Islam and Indian History* (Princeton: Princeton University Press, 1978); Muzaffar Alam, *The Languages of Political Islam* and *The Mughals and the Sufis* (Ranikhet: Permanent Black, 2004).
4. Nile Green, *Indian Sufism since the Seventeenth Century* (Oxon and New York: Routledge, 2006); *Making Space: Sufis and Settlers in Early Modern India* (New Delhi: Oxford University Press, 2012); S. Kugle, 'Sufi Attitude toward Homosexuality'; 'The Chishtiyya';

Mitto Viitamäki, 'Retelling Medieval History for Twentieth-century Readers' in *Literary and Religious Practices in Medieval and Early Modern India*, edited by Raziuddin Aquil and David L. Curley (New Delhi: New Delhi and London: Manohar and Routledge, 2016). Also see Raziuddin Aquil, *Sufism, Culture, and Politics* (Oxford University Press, 2007); *Lovers of God* (New Delhi and London: Manohar and Routledge, 2017).

5. I. H. Qureshi, *Ulema in Politics* (New Delhi: Renaissance Publishing House, 1985); Aziz Ahmad, *Studies in Islamic Culture* (Oxford: Clarendon Press, 1964).
6. K. S. Lal, *The Legacy of Muslim Rule in India* (New Delhi: Aditya Prakashan, 1992).
7. Peter Jackson, *The Delhi Sultanate* (New York: Cambridge University Press, 1999); Sunil Kumar, *The Emergence of the Delhi Sultanate* (Ranikhet: Permanent Black, 2007); Blain H. Auer, *Symbols of Authority in Medieval Islam* (London and New York I. B. Tauris, 2012); *In the Mirror of Persian Kings* (Cambridge: Cambridge University Press, 2021). Also see Catherine B. Asher and Cynthia Talbot, *India before Europe* (United Kingdom: Cambridge University Press, 2006).
8. For Deccani Sultanates, see Richard M. Eaton and Phillip B. Wagoner, *Power, Memory, Architecture* (New Delhi: Oxford University Press, 2013); Emma J. Flatt, *The Court of the Deccan Sultanates* (Cambridge:

Cambridge University Press, 2019). For Mughal India, see Habib, *The Agrarian System of Mughal India* (Bombay: Asia Publishing House, 1963); M. Athar Ali, *Mughal India* (New Delhi: Oxford University Press, 2006); Iqtidar Alam Khan, *Akbar and His Age* (New Delhi: Northern Book Centre, 1999); Harbans Mukhia, *Historians and Historiography During the Reign of Akbar* (New Delhi: Vikas Publishing House, 1976); Muzaffar Alam, Sanjay Subrahmanyam, *The Mughal State, 1526–1750* (New Delhi: Oxford University Press, 1998). The best of the research is now being conducted in the United States of America, for which the early exemplars include John F. Richards, *The Mughal Empire* (Cambridge: Cambridge University Press, 1993).

9. Minhaj Siraj Juzjani, *Tabaqat-i-Nasiri* (Calcutta: Asiatic Society of Bengal, 1881); Ziauddin Barani, *Tarikh-i-Firuz Shahi*, tr. Ishtiaq Ahmad Zilli (New Delhi: Primus Books, 2015) and *Fatawa-i-Jahandari*; Amir Khusrau, *Khaza'in-ul-Futuh*, ed. M. Wahid Mirza (Calcutta: Asiatic Society, 1953) Also see M. Wahid Mirza, *Amir Khusrau* (Delhi: National Amir Khusrau Society, 1986); Sunil Sharma, *Amir Khusraw* (Oxford: Oneworld Academic, 2005).
10. Important examples of such texts include: Abul Hasan Ali bin Hujwiri, *Kashf-ul-Mahjub*; Sijzi, *Fawa'id-ul-Fu'ad*; Kirmani, *Siyar-ul-Auliya*; Sharf-ud-Din Yahya Maneri, *Maktubat-i-Sadi*; Dehlawi, *Akhbar-ul-Akhyar.*

11. For some good uses of the *premakhyana* such as *Chandayan, Madhumalati* and *Padmavat,* see Madhu Trivedi, *Revisiting Hindavi Sufi Romances: Late Fourteenth to Early Sixteenth Centuries* (New Delhi: Primus Books, 2024); Aditya Behl, *Emotion and Meaning in Mrigavat?: Strategies of Spiritual Signification in Hindavi Sufi Romances* (New Delhi: Oxford University Press, 2014); Ramya Sreenivasan, *The Many Lives of a Rajput Queen* (United States: University of Washington Press, 2007).
12. For accounts of the lives and activities around these important figures in Chishti Sufism, see P. M. Currie, *The Shrine and Cult of Mu'īn Al-Dīn Chishtī of Ajmer* (New Delhi: Oxford University Press, 1989); Simon Digby, 'Early Pilgrimages to the graves of Mu'in al-Din Sijzi and other Indian Chishti Shaykhs' *Islamic Society and Culture – Essays in Honour of Aziz Ahmad,* eds, M. Israel and N. K. Wagle (New Delhi: Manohar, 1983); Nizami, *The Life and Times of Shaikh Nizamuddin Auliya.*
13. From a vast body of critical literature on Sufism, generally, see Annemarie Schimmel, *Mystical Dimensions of Islam* (Chapel Hill: University of North Carolina Press, 1975); William C. Chittick, *Sufism: A Short Introduction* (Oxford: Oneworld Publications, 2008); Ahmet T. Karamustafa, *Sufism: The Formative Period* (Edinburgh: Edinburgh University Press, 2007). Also see Raziuddin Aquil (ed.), *Sufism and Society in Medieval India* (New Delhi: Oxford University Press, 2010).

14. For some relevant discussion, see Digby, 'Qalandars and Related Groups'; Matthew Clark, 'Religious Sects, Syncretism, and Claims of Antiquity: The Dashanami-Sannyasis and South Asian Sufis', *Literary and Religious Practices in Medieval and Early Modern India*, eds. Raziuddin Aquil, David L. Curley (New Delhi and London: Manohar and Routledge, 2016).
15. For a detailed analysis of the controversy, see Aquil, *Lovers of God.*
16. Ruth Vanita, *The Dharma of Justice in the Sanskrit Epics: Debates on Gender, Varna, and Species* (New Delhi: Oxford University Press, 2022); Eleanor Zelliot, *A Medieval Encounter between Hindu and Muslim: Eknath's Drama-poem Hindu-turk samvad.* in Fred Clothey, ed., *Images of Man: Religion and Historical Process in South Asia, Madras: New Era, 1982* (New Delhi: Oxford University Press, 2003), pp. 64-82.

2. Kinder Face of Islam

1. Sijzi, *Fawa'id-ul-Fu'ad*, p. 305
2. Ibid., p. 148.
3. Kirmani, *Siyar-ul-Auliya*, p. 165.

3. Ethical Excellence Amidst the Ugliness of the World

1. Sijzi, *Fawa'id-ul-Fu'ad*, pp. 155–57.
2. Ibid., p. 84.

3. Ibid., pp. 35–36, 416–18.
4. Ibid., p. 325.
5. Ibid., pp. 106–07.

4. Fasting and Feasting

1. Sijzi, *Fawa'id-ul-Fu'ad.*
2. Sijzi, *Fawa'id-ul-Fu'ad*, pp. 130, 234.
3. Ibid., pp. 158–9.
4. Ibid.
5. Kirmani, *Siyar-ul-Auliya*, pp. 160–1.
6. Muzaffar Alam, *The Mughals and the Sufis: Islam and Political Imagination in India, 1500–1750* (Ranikhet: Permanent Black, 2021).
7. Sijzi, *Fawa'id-ul-Fu'ad*, pp. 12–13.
8. Ibid., pp. 16–17.
9. Ibid., p. 91. *Harise*, mentioned in the couplet, was a type of thick pottage made from crushed wheat, boiled to a consistency to which meat, butter, cinnamon and aromatic herbs were added; see F. A. *A Comprehensive Persian-English Dictionary* (New Delhi: Munshiram Manoharlal, 1996), p. 1, 497. This appears similar to the now strong and popular dish called *halim*.
10. Sijzi, *Fawa'id-ul-Fu'ad*, p. 12.
11. Ibid., p. 17.
12. Ibid., p. 4.
13. Ibid., p. 30.
14. Ibid., p. 33.
15. Ibid., p. 8.

16. Ibid., p. 10.
17. Ibid., p. 40.
18. Ibid., p. 48.
19. Dehlawi, *Akhbar-ul-Akhyar*.
20. *Siyar-ul-Auliya* refers to serious harassment of the Sufi saint by Sultan Muhammad Tughluq, which the former attributed to God's wisdom, such as checking on the limits of his patience and determination to continue on the righteous path, see Kirmani, *Siyar-ul-Auliya*, pp. 255–6. For a modern biography of the Sufi saint, see Nizami, *The Life and Times of Shaikh Nasiruddin Chiragh*.
21. Sijzi, *Fawa'id-ul-Fu'ad*, p. 65.
22. Jon Keune, *Shared Devotion, Shared Food: Equality and the Bhakti-Caste Question in Western India* (New York: Oxford University Press, 2021).

5. Merits of Feeding the Poor

1. For an interesting discussion on sharing food as an important strand of Marathi Bhakti tradition, see Keune, *Shared Devotion, Shared Food*. For some relevant discussion, see Jayanta Sengupta, 'The History and Historiography of Indian Food: The State of the Field', *Food Cultures of India* (New Delhi: Manohar, 2024).
2. Sijzi, *Fawa'id-ul-Fu'ad*.
3. Richard C. Foltz, *Animals in Islamic Tradition and Muslim Cultures* (Oxford: Oneworld, 2006), p. 133.
4. Dehlawi, *Akhbar-ul-Akhyar*.

5. Linda Hess and Sukhdev Singh, *The Bijak of Kabir* (New Delhi: Motilal Banarsidass, 2000); Charlotte Vaudeville, *A Weaver Named Kabir – Selected Verses with a Detailed Biographical and Historical Introduction* (New Delhi: Oxford University Press, 1993); John S. Hawley, *A Storm of Songs: India and the Idea of the Bhakti Movement* (Cambridge, MA: Harvard University Press, 2015); David Lorenzen, *Nirgun Santon Ke Swapana* (New Delhi: Rajkamal, 2010); Ruth Vanita, *The Dharma of Justice in the Sanskrit Epic: Debates on Gender, Varna, and Species* (Oxford: Oxford University Press, 2022); Madhav Hada, *Kabir: Kaaljayi Kavi aur Unka Kavya* (New Delhi: Rajpal and Sons, 2022).
6. Abir Bazaz, *Nund Rishi: Poetry and Politics in Medieval Kashmir* (Cambridge: Cambridge University Press, 2023); Chitralekha Zutshi, *Kashmir's Contested Pasts: Narratives, Sacred Geographies and the Historical Imagination* (New Delhi: Oxford University Press, 2014); Yohannan Friedmann, *Shaykh Ahmed Sirhindi: An Outline of His Thought and a Study of His Image in the Eyes of Posterity* (Ontario: McGill–Queen's University Press, 1972).
7. Ziya Us Salam, *Lynch Files: The Forgotten Saga of Victims of Hate Crime* (New Delhi: Sage, 2019). For a recent analysis of an older attempt at studied 'vegetarianization', see Andrea Gutiérrez, 'Meat on and off the Royal Menu: The Medieval Delight of the Mind & the Erasure of Meat from Indian Recipe Collections', *Global Food History* vol. 10,

no. 2, 1972, pp. 140–58. Julia Hauser, *A Taste for Purity: An Entangled History of Vegetarianism* (New York: Columbia University Press, 2024) tracks the connected history of vegetarianism in India and abroad for a century between the middle of the nineteenth century to the middle of the twentieth. Mahatma Gandhi's vegetarianism is also dragged into this conversation some time. Amar Farooqui, 'Gandhi's Spiritual Politics: Austerity, Fasting and Secularism', *Studies in History*, vol. 36, no. 2, 2020, pp. 178–205 has suggested that Gandhi did not advocate surveillance of kitchens, nor did he try to impose his food preferences, and he would have opposed the use of the state for prohibition.

8. Sijzi, *Fawa'id-ul-Fu'ad*, pp. 53–4.
9. Nuzhat Kazmi, *Mughal Art of Portraiture, Awraq-eMusavvir, The Intellectual Context and Content* (New Delhi: Three Essays Collective, 2021).
10. Ibid., pp. 27–8. For great symbolic significance of food in the heart of different religious traditions, see Keune, *Shared Devotion, Shared Food*, p. 104. Also see Corrie E. Norman, 'Food and Religion', *The Oxford Handbook of Food History* (Oxford: Oxford University Press, 2012), pp. 409–27.
11. Sijzi, *Fawa'id-ul-Fu'ad*, p. 63.
12. Qiwam, *Qiwam-ul-'Aqa'id.*
13. Trivedi, *Revisiting Hindavi Sufi Romance*, pp. 145–9.
14. Ibid., pp. 155–9.
15. Kirmani, *Siyar-ul-Auliya.*

6. Respect for Women

1. For more detailed explanations of the evolution of these features of Sufism, see Karamustafa, *Sufism*; Chittick, *Sufism*; Hujwiri, *Kashf-ul-Mahjub* remains the oldest classic text on Sufi theory.
2. Sijzi, *Fawa'id-ul-Fu'ad*, p. 35.
3. Hujwiri, *Kashf-ul-Mahjub*, p. 526.
4. Dehlawi, *Akhbar-ul-Akhyar*, pp. 582–5; Sijzi, *Fawa'id-ul-Fu'ad*, pp. 35–6, 416–18.
5. Muqtedar Khan and Mohammed Ayub Khan, 'Poverty in Islamic Philosophy', in *The Routledge Handbook of Philosophy and Poverty*, ed. Gottfried Schweiger and Clemens Sedmak (New York: Routledge, 2023)
6. Scott Kugle, 'The Chishtiyya', in *The Routledge Handbook on Sufism*, ed. Lloyd Ridgeon (London: Routledge, 2020).
7. Sijzi, *Fawa'id-ul-Fu'ad*, pp. 35–6, 415–7. In another context, a learned scholar of Lahore (now in Pakistan) claimed he had a deep aspiration and desire (*arzu* and *ishtiyaq*) to see the Ka'ba in Mecca, Arabia, and wanted permission from the local custodian of Islam, the *qazi*, to travel; the latter retorted that if he were truly determined, permission was not required; he would just hit the road (*na ijajazat talabidi o na mashawarat kardi mi rafti*). Narrating this, Nizamuddin remarked that in matters of love, no permission or consultation was required (*dar ishq mashawarat nist*).

8. Kirmani, *Siyar-ul-Auliya*, p. 98. For a report on how the family lost her in a jungle on the way from Delhi to Ajodhan, see Dehlawi, *Akhbar-ul-Akhyar*, pp. 585–6.
9. For a detailed biographical sketch of Bibi Zulaikha, see Dehlawi, *Akhbar-ul-Akhyar*, pp. 586–8.
10. Dehlawi, *Akhbar-ul-Akhyar*, p. 582.
11. Sijzi, *Fawa'id-ul-Fu'ad*, p. 438.
12. For a long history of Chishti Sufism, see Ernst and Lawrence, *Sufi Martyrs of Love*.
13. Dehlawi, *Akhbar-ul-Akhyar*, p. 588.
14. Hujwiri, *Kashf-ul-Mahjub*, p. 530.
15. Ibid., p. 531.
16. Emil Homerin, *Aisha al-Ba'uniyya: A Life in Praise of Love* (London: Oneworld Academic, 2019).
17. Sijzi, *Fawa'id-ul-Fu'ad*, p. 323.

7. Miracle as a Source of Benevolence

1. Sijzi, *Fawa'id-ul-Fu'ad,* p. 116.
2. Hamid Qalandar, *Khair-ul-Majalis,* Conversations of Shaikh Nasiruddin Chiragh-i-Dehli, ed. K. A. Nizami (Aligarh: Muslim University, 1959), thirty-fifth Meeting.
3. Sijzi, *Fawa'id-ul-Fu'ad*, pp. 100–1.
4. Ibid., p. 116.
5. Ibid., pp. 79–80.
6. Kirmani, *Siyar-ul-Auliya*, p. 135.
7. *Khair-ul-Majalis,* thirty-third meeting. For such struggles over the dead body of medieval Christianity, see Aron Gurevich, *Medieval Popular*

Culture: Problems of Belief and Perception (Cambridge: Cambridge University Press, 1988), p. 39.

8. For the healing power of a relic of Shaikh Farid, see Sijzi, *Fawa'id-ul-Fu'ad*, pp. 106–7; Kirmani, *Siyar-ul-Auliya*, pp. 173–4; Shaikh Jamali, *Siyar-ul-Arifin*, pp. 68–9. For the *barkat* or blessings accrued from the tank constructed by Sultan Shamsuddin Iltutmish in collaboration with Khwaja Qutbuddin Bakhtiyar Kaki, see Sijzi, *Fawa'id-ul-Fu'ad*, p. 205.
9. Jamali, *Siyar-ul-Arifin*, p. 95.
10. Sijzi, *Fawa'id-ul-Fu'ad*, p. 336.
11. Sudhir Kakar, *Shamans, Mystics and Doctors: A Psychological Inquiry into India and Its Healing Traditions* (New Delhi: Oxford University Press, 1982), p. 29.
12. Qiwam, *Qiwam-ul-Aqa'id*, pp. 38–40.
13. Sijzi, *Fawa'id-ul-Fu'ad*, p. 195.
14. Ibid., pp. 106–07.
15. Ibid., pp. 247–48, 316.
16. Ibid., pp. 243–4.
17. Ibid., p. 374.
18. Izzuddin Isami, *Futuh-us-Salatin* vol. III, tr. Agha Mahdi Husain (Bombay: Asia Publishing House, 1977), pp. 687–8.

8. Encounters with Opponents

1. Hazrat Badruddin Ishaq, *Asrar-ul-Auliya*, collection of the *malfuzat* of Fariduddin Ganj-i-Shakar, tr. Abdus Sami Zia (Sahiwal: Maktaba-i-Faridiya,

1978), p. 188; Kirmani, *Siyar-ul-Auliya*, pp. 180–2; Jamali, *Siyar-ul-Arifin*, p. 50.

2. Kirmani, *Siyar-ul-Auliya*, p. 64.
3. Ibid., p. 145.
4. Ibid., p. 143–5.
5. Qiwam, *Qiwam-ul-Aqa'id*, pp. 91–6. Also see Jamali, *Siyar-ul-Arifin*, pp. 99–100, 105–06; Barani, *Tarikh-i-Firuz Shahi*, p. 503.
6. Kirmani, *Siyar-ul-Auliya*, pp. 255–56. For an analysis of this episode, see Simon Digby, 'The Sufi Shaikh and the Sultan: A Conflict of Claims to Authority in Medieval India', *Journal of Persian Studies* vol. 28, 1990, p. 74.
7. For important discussion on the authority connotation of the Sufi shaikh's *wilayat*, leading to conflict with the rulers and the victory of the shaikh as recorded in the sources of the Delhi Sultanate, see Digby, 'The Sufi Shaikh and the Sultan', pp. 71–4.
8. Qiwam, *Qiwam-ul-Aqa'id*, p. 52.
9. Ibid., pp. 98–9.
10. *Khair-ul-Majalis*, eighty-seventh meeting.
11. Kirmani, *Siyar-ul-Auliya*, p. 160.
12. Ibid., p. 161.
13 Jamali, *Siyar-ul-Arifin*, p. 100–1.
14. Ibid., p. 102–3.
15. Ibid., p. 103–5.
16. Barani, *Tarikh-i-Firuz Shahi*, pp. 571–88.

9. Defence of Sufi Music

1. For the couplet cited above, see Sijzi, *Fawa'id-ul-Fu'ad*, p. 312. For a good introduction to the early phase of Sufism, see Karamustafa, *Sufism*; Chittick, *Sufism*. For a general history of Chishti Sufism, see Ernst and Lawrence, *Sufi Martyrs of Love*. For discussion of relevant issues, also see Aquil (ed.), *Sufism and Society in Medieval India*.
2. Kirmani, *Siyar-ul-Auliya*, p. 645.
3. Ibid., p. 646; Sijzi, *Fawa'id-ul-Fu'ad*, pp. 418–19.
4. Sijzi, *Fawa'id-ul-Fu'ad*, p. 419.
5. Kirmani, *Siyar-ul-Auliya*, p. 647.
6. Ibid., p. 648.
7. Ibid., pp. 648–49.
8. Ibid., p. 658; Sijzi, *Fawa'id-ul-Fu'ad*, p. 419.
9. Kirmani, *Siyar-ul-Auliya*, p. 658.
10. Ibid., pp. 664–5.
11. Ibid., pp. 662, 665.
12. Ibid., pp. 666–7.
13. Ibid., pp. 667–8.
14. Ibid., p. 686.
15. Ibid., p. 687.
16. Ibid.
17. Ibid., p. 688.
18. Ibid.
19. Ibid., pp. 688–9.
20. Ibid., p. 689–90.
21. Ibid., p. 690.
22. Ibid., pp. 690–1.

23. Ibid., p. 691.
24. Sijzi, *Fawa'id-ul-Fu'ad*, p. 384.
25. Ibid., pp. 384–5.
26. Ibid., pp. 385–6.
27. Ibid., p. 386.
28. Jamali, *Siyar-ul-Arifin*, fols. 97b–99b. Ziyauddin Barani refers to the recovery of the amount distributed by Khusrau Khan, but makes no mention of Nizamuddin Auliya in this context; see Barani, *Tarikh-i-Firuz Shahi*, British Museum Ms. 6376, fols. 199b–200a.
29. For the bestowal of kingship upon the prince shortly before the death of the sultan, see Qiwam, *Qiwam-ul-Aqa'id*, p. 96. Ibn Battuta, tr. Maulwi Muhammad Husain, *Aja'ib-ul-Asfar*, Urdu translation (Islamabad, 1983), p. 92. For Barani's account of the ruler's accidental death, see Barani, *Tarikh-i-Firuz Shahi*, fols. 209b–210a.
30. Hujwiri, *Kashf-ul-Mahjub*.
31. Sijzi, *Fawa'id-ul-Fu'ad*, p. 385.

10. Recitation of Persian Poetry

1. Sijzi, *Fawa'id-ul-Fu'ad*, p. 216.
2. Ibid., pp. 226–7.
3. Ibid., p. 227.
4. Ibid., pp. 173–4.
5. Ibid., p. 174.
6. Ibid., pp. 254–5.
7. Ibid., p. 255.

8. Dehlawi, *Akhbar-ul-Akhyar*, p. 115.
9. Sijzi, *Fawa'id-ul-Fu'ad*, p. 246.
10. Dehlawi, *Akhbar-ul-Akhyar*, pp. 114–15.
11. Sijzi, *Fawa'id-ul-Fu'ad*, p. 301.
12. Tr. Ziya-ul-Hasan Faruqi, *Fawa'id al-Fu'ad: Spiritual and Literary Discourses of Shaikh Nizamuddin Auliya*, originally compiled by Amir Hasan 'Ala' Sijzi Dehlawi (New Delhi: D. K. Printworld, 1996), pp. 334–5.
13. Sijzi, *Fawa'id-ul-Fu'ad*, p. 169.
14. Ibid., p. 169.
15. Ibid., p. 170.
16. Ibid., pp. 423–24.
17. Ibid., p. 342.

11. Following the Path of the Prophet

1. Sijzi, *Fawa'id-ul-Fu'ad*, p. 424; Faruqi, *Fawa'id al-Fu'ad*, p. 441.
2. Ibid., pp. 175–6; pp. 226–7.
3. Ibid., p. 177; pp. 227–8.
4. Ibid., p. 177; p. 228.
5. Ibid., pp. 177–8; p. 228.
6. Ibid., pp. 178–9; p. 229.
7. Ibid., p. 179; p. 229.
8. Ibid., pp. 180–1; p. 230.
9. Ibid., p. 181; pp. 230–1.
10. Ibid., p. 151; p. 203.
11. Ibid., pp. 395–6; p. 417.
12. Ibid., p. 396; p. 417.

13. Ibid., pp. 396–7; pp. 417–18.
14. Ibid., p. 198; pp. 245–6.
15. Ibid., p. 198; p. 246.
16. Ibid., pp. 199–200; p. 247.
17. Ibid., p. 200; p. 247.
18. Ibid., p. 200; p. 248.

12. Attitude Towards Conversion and Islamicization

1. Raziuddin Aquil, 'Sufi Cults, Politics and Conversion: The Chishtis of the Sultanate Period', *Indian Historical Review,* vol. 22, nos. 1–2, 1995–96, pp. 190–97.
2. Simon Digby, 'Hawk and Dove in Sufi Combat', *Pembroke Papers 1,* Cambridge, 1990, pp. 7–25; 'To Ride a Tiger or a Wall? Strategies of Prestige in Indian Sufi Legend', *According to Tradition: Hagiographical Writing in India* (Wiesbaden: Otto Harrassowitz, 1994), pp. 99–129.
3. Josep Marti I Perez, 'Encountering the Irrational: Some Reflections on Folk Healers', *Folklore* vol. 99, No. 2, 1988, pp. 178–5; Richard Kieckhefer, 'The Specific Rationality of Medieval Magic', *American Historical Review,* 1994 vol. 3, pp. 813–36.
4. Caroline Walker Bynum, 'Wonder', *American Historical Review* vol. 102, no. 1, 1997, p. 17.
5. Ibid., pp. 17–18.
6. K. A. Nizami, *The Life and Times of Shaikh Fariduddin Ganj-i-Shakar* (Aligarh: Muslim University, 1955), p.

107; Bruce B. Lawrence, 'Early Indo-Muslim Saints and Conversion', *Islam in Asia* vol. I, 1984, p. 110.

7. For biographical notices, Dehlawi, *Akhbar-ul-Akhyar,* pp. 43–5; Rizvi, *History of Sufism in India* vol. I, pp. 199–202.
8. For biographical material, Dehlawi, *Akhbar-ul-Akhyar,* pp. 161–2; Rizvi, *History of Sufism in India,* Vol. I, pp. 266–70.
9. Lawrence, 'Early Indo-Muslim Saints and Conversion', p. 116.
10. Amir Khusrau, *Afzal-ul-Fawa'id,* collection of the discourses of Nizam–ud–Din Auliya, Urdu translation (New Delhi: Maktaba Jame Noor), p. 13. For more anecdotes of the gold production motif in Sufi literature, see Shaikh Fariduddin Ganj-i-Shakar, *Fawa'id-us-Salikin,* conversations of Khwaja Qutbuddin Bakhtiyar Kaki, Urdu translation (New Delhi: Maktaba Jame Noor), p. 15; *Rahat-ul-Qulub,* p. 82; Khusrau, *Afzal-ul-Fawa'id,* pp. 32–3, 102, 126; Ishaq, *Asrar-ul-Auliya,* p. 202.
11. For an English translation of the anecdote, see I. H. Siddiqui, *Perso-Arabic Sources of Information on the Life and Conditions in the Sultanate of Delhi* (New Delhi: Munshiram Manoharlal, 1992), pp. 13–14. For this anecdote, also see *Tazkirat-ul-Auliya,* Part I, p. 76.
12. Khusrau, *Afzal-ul-Fawa'id,* pp. 20–1. Another version of this anecdote is recorded in *Tazkirat-ul-Auliya,* where the neighbour of the shaikh is referred to as a *gabri* (Magian).

13. Sijzi, *Fawa'id-ul-Fu'ad* vol. II, twenty-third meeting.
14. Kirmani, *Siyar-ul-Auliya*, p. 168.
15. Jamali, *Siyar-ul-Arifin*, p. 16.
16. Khusrau, *Afzal-ul-Fawa'id*, p. 50.
17. Compare to K. A. Nizami's statement that miracle-mongering had no place in the spiritual discipline of Nizamuddin Auliya. Introduction, *Fawa'id-ul-Fu'ad*, tr. Bruce B. Lawrence, *Nizamuddin Auliya: Morals for the Heart, Conversations of Shaikh Nizamuddin Auliya recorded by Amir Hasan Sijzi* (New York: Paulist Press, 1992), p. 15.
18. Digby, 'Sufi Shaikh as a Source of Authority', pp. 69–70.
19. Sijzi, *Fawa'id-ul-Fu'ad* vol. II, fifth meeting.
20. *Khair-ul-Majalis*, eleventh meeting
21. Sijzi, *Fawa'id-ul-Fu'ad* vol. 1, twenty-eighth meeting. Also see Dehlawi, *Akhbar-ul-Akhyar*, p. 53, where Abdul Haq refers to Fariduddin Ganj-i-Shakar's *malfuzat* collected by Nizamuddin Auliya.

13. Excellence of Disciples

1. For important modern accounts of Amir Khusrau's life and works, see Mirza, *Amir Khusrau*; Sharma, *Amir Khusraw.*
2. For Khusrau's life in medieval biographies, see Kirmani, *Siyar-ul-Auliya*, pp. 308–12; Dehlawi, *Akhbar-ul-Akhyar*, pp. 215–18.
3. Dehlawi, *Akhbar-ul-Akhyar*, pp. 215–16.

4. Kirmani, *Siyar-ul-Auliya*, p. 309; Dehlawi, *Akhbar-ul-Akhyar*, pp. 215–16.
5. Kirmani, *Siyar-ul-Auliya*, p. 308.
6. Dehlawi, *Akhbar-ul-Akhyar*, pp. 216.
7. Kirmani, *Siyar-ul-Auliya*, p. 311; Dehlawi, *Akhbar-ul-Akhyar*, pp. 218.
8. Barani, *Tarikh-i-Firuz Shahi*, p. 221.
9. Ibid., pp. 221–2.
10. Dehlawi, *Akhbar-ul-Akhyar*, pp. 2018–19.
11. Ibid., p. 219.
12. Ibid., p. 219.
13. Ibid., p. 221.
14. Ibid., p. 220.
15. Barani, *Tarikh-i-Firuz Shahi*, p. 222.
16. Ibid., p. 222.
17. Ibid.
18. Sijzi, *Fawa'id-ul-Fu'ad*, p. 369.
19. Barani, *Tarikh-i-Firuz Shahi*, p. 15.
20. Kirmani, *Siyar-ul-Auliya*, pp. 319–20.
21. Ibid., p. 320.
22. Barani, *Tarikh-i-Firuz Shahi*, p. 209.
23. Ibid., pp. 210–12.
24. Ibid., pp. 212–13.
25. Ibid., p. 213.

14. The Glorious Chishti Tradition

1. Kirmani, *Siyar-ul-Auliya*.
2. Ibid.
3. Khwaja Qutbuddin Bakhtiyar Kaki, *Dalil-ul-'Arifin*, conversations of Khwaja Muinuddin Chishti, Urdu

translation (New Delhi: Maktaba Jame Noor); Ganj-i-Shakar, *Fawa'id-us-Salikin*.

4. Ishaq, *Asrar-ul-Auliya*.
5. Sijzi, *Fawa'id-ul-Fu'ad*, p. 405.
6. Khwaja Moinuddin Chishti Ajmeri, *Anis-ul-Arwah*, collection of the discourses of Usman Harwani, Urdu translation (New Delhi: Maktaba Jame Noor), p. 45.
7. Kaki, *Dalil-ul-Arifin*, pp. 10–13, 30, 42.
8. Ganj-i-Shakar, *Fawa'id-us-Salikin*, p. 26; Kaki, *Dalil-ul-Arifin,* p. 40. For more anecdotes of the Ka'ba visiting a Sufi shaikh and circumambulating him, Ajmeri, *Anis-ul-Arwah*, p. 12; Ganj-i-Shakar, *Fawa'id-us-Salikin*, p. 26.
9. Kirmani, *Siyar-ul-Auliya,* pp. 56–7.
10. Ibid.
11. Dehlawi, *Akhbar-ul-Akhyar*, pp. 56–7.
12. Ibid., p. 56.
13. Mughal princess Jahanara Begam in her *Munis-ul-Arwah*, as quoted by Nausheen Jaffrey, *Jahan Ara Begum* (New Delhi: Tulika Books, 2025), p. 129.
14. Ibid. p. 129.
15. Sijzi, *Fawa'id-ul-Fu'ad*, p. 246.
16. Kirmani, *Siyar-ul-Auliya*.
17. Ibid., pp. 69–71.
18. Raziuddin Aquil, 'Episodes from the Life of Shaikh Farid-ud-Din Ganj-i-Shakar', *International Journal of Punjab Studies* vol. 10, nos. 1–2, 2003, pp. 25–46. For a full-length modern biography, see Nizami, *The Life and Times of Shaikh Fariduddin Ganj-i-Shakar*.

19. Ali Asghar, *Jawahir-i-Faridi* (Lahore: Victoria Press), p. 185.
20. Dehlawi, *Akhbar-ul-Akhyar*, p. 51.
21. Aquil, 'Episodes from the Life of Shaikh Farid-ud-Din Ganj-i-Shakar'.
22. Kirmani, *Siyar-ul-Auliya*, pp. 249–50; Dehlawi, *Akhbar-ul-Akhyar*, pp. 177–8.
23. For detailed references to the significant role of Shaikh Farid in the emergence of Muslim Punjabi culture, see Aquil, 'Episodes from the Life of Shaikh Farid-ud-Din Ganj-i-Shakar'.
24. Kirmani, *Siyar-ul-Auliya*, p. 247.
25. Ibid., p. 247.
26. *Khair-ul-Majalis*, pp. 247–56. Dehlawi, *Akhbar-ul-Akhyar*, pp. 176–90. Also see K. A. Nizami, *Life and Times of Shaikh Nasiruddin Chiragh* (Delhi: Idarah-i Adabiyat-i Delli, 1991b).
27. Kirmani, *Siyar-ul-Auliya*, p. 256; Abdul Haq Muhaddis adds that in tolerating the harassment, Nasiruddin was following the advice of Hazrat Nizamuddin not to run away from the demands of the time, Dehlawi, *Akhabr-ul-Akhyar*, p. 178.
28. Dehlawi, *Akhbar-ul-Akhyar*, p. 178.
29. Kirmani, *Siyar-ul-Auliya*, p. 256.
30. Ibid., p. 257.
31. Dehlawi, *Akhbar-ul-Akhyar*, pp. 180–1.

15. Conclusion: Extraordinary Lover of God

1. Sijzi, *Fawa'id-ul-Fu'ad*, p. 243.
2. Ibid., p. 376.

GLOSSARY OF TERMS

Abdaal: Men of the invisible world

Alam-i-ghaib: World of the unseen

Anal Haq: I am the Truth (attributed to Sufi practitioner, Mansur al-Hallaj)

Aql: Intellect

Azaan: Call for prayers

Baba: Spiritual figure

Bhakti: Complete devotion to God

Bismillah: In the name of Allah

Buzurg: A saintly person, such as a Sufi

Chilla-i-ma'kus: Inverted *chilla* or meditation for forty nights by hanging upside down, practised by some Sufis

Dargah: A large Sufi shrine, tomb

Darbar: Sufi shrines or courts of medieval rulers

Dozakh: Hell

Faqir: Mendicant, dervish, poor

Farman: Royal order or command

Fatiha: Prayer

Fatwa: A judicial decree pronounced by a Muslim *mufti*, for whom see below

Fiqh: Islamic jurisprudence

Firqa: Sect, community

Fitna: Sedition, anarchy, calamity, discord

Futuh: Alms received by Sufis as unasked-for charity

Ghazal: Poetry of love

Gunah: Sin

Guru: Spiritual leader

Haal: Spiritual feeling of ecstasy

Hadis: Traditions associated with Prophet Muhammad

Hajj: Pilgrimage to Mecca in Arabia

Halal: Permissible, allowed in Islam

Hamd: Poetry in praise of God

Haqiqat: Truth of the loving God

Haram: Forbidden, unlawful in Islam

Hikayat: Anecdotes or stories

Ishq: Love

Istidraj: Paranormal abilities of non-Muslim mystics, such as the *yogis*

Jadu: Magic

Jagir: Land assignment

Jalal: Wrathful, mighty power

Jama'at-khana: Sufi hospice smaller than *khanaqah* (for which see below)

Jamal: Elegant, graceful

Jizya: Capitation tax, initially paid by Jews and Christians in an Islamic regime

Kafir: Infidel

Karamat: Miracle performed by Sufi saints

Khalifa: Spiritual successor of a Sufi, caliph

Khanaqah: Large Sufi hospice

Khayal: A form of Hindustani classical music, named after imagination or meditation

Khutba: Sermon, especially preached in the mosques on Fridays

Khwaja: Sufi master descended from the family of Prophet Muhammad

Langar: Sufi practice of serving food in their hospices, *khanaqah* or *jama'at-khana*

Makruh: Abominable

Maktubat: Letters (written by Sufis to their disciples)

Malfuzat: Spiritual conversations of Sufis

Mannat: Blessings and benedictions sought by visitors at Sufi shrines

Ma'rifat: Spiritual knowledge

Maslak: Sect or creed

Ma'unat: Low-quality tricks, magic and other evils (*jadu*)

Mazar: Grave

Mazhab: Religion, school of jurisprudence in Islamic traditions (plural: *mazahib*)

Mu'ajizat: Marvels of the prophets

Mubah: Permissible

Muezzin: The person who proclaims the calls for prayer in mosques

Mufti: Expounder of Muslim law, giver of *fatwa*

Muhaddis: Scholar of traditions of the Prophet

Muhtasib: Censor official

Murtadd: Apostate

Na'at: Poetry in praise of the Prophet of Islam

Namaz: Muslim form of worship

Nazar: Evil eye

Nirgun: Devotion for a formless God

Panth: Community of the Sikhs

Pir: Sufi master

Pranayama: Yogic breath control

Premakhyana: Poetry of love

Qalb: Heart

Qasida: An elegy, a poem of praise

Qawwali: Singing and playing musical instruments in Sufi traditions

Qayamat: Day of Judgement in Islam

Qazi: Judge

Raqs: Dance

Roza: Fasting

Rizq: Means of sustenance

Sama: Musical assembly of Sufis (*mahfil-i-sama* or *majlis-i-sama*)

Sagun: Worship or devotion for God with form

Sanyasi: An ascetic or religious mendicant

Sarod: Musical instrument

Shaikh: Sufi master

Shahid: Martyr

Shari'at: Islamic law

Silsila: Sufi order, or spiritual genealogy

Sitar: Musical instrument

Sufi: Muslim mystic

Sulh-i kul: Peace with all, perfect or absolute peace

Surur: Sufi experience of cheerfulness, exhilaration

Tabarruk: Sacred relic or food items

Taqwa: Piety

Tariqat: Sufi path or practice

Tark-i-duniya: Sufis' renunciation of the world

Tauba: Repentance

Tauhid: The concept of the unity of God in Islam

Ta'wiz: Amulet

Tawakkul: Complete trust in God

Tazkira: Hagiographical or biographical dictionaries

Tazkiya-i-nafs: Cleansing of the lower self of one's body

Ulama: Muslim religious scholars (singular: *alim*)

Umma: Community of Muslims

Urs: Death anniversary of Sufis

Wahdat-ul-wujud: Unity of existence

Wahdat-us-shuhud: Unity of witness

Wali: A friend of God (*Waliullah*)

Wilayat: Spiritual territory (of Sufis), also territories controlled by rulers

Zakat: Obligatory payment of tax by Muslims of sufficient means

BIBLIOGRAPHY

Aftab, Tahira. *Sufi Women of South Asia: Veiled Friends of God*, first published by Brill, Leiden, in 2022 (New Delhi: Manohar, 2025).

Ahmad, Aziz. *Studies in Islamic Culture in Indian Environment* (Oxford: Clarendon Press, 1964).

Akhbar-ul-Akhyar of Shaikh Abdul Haq Muhaddis Dehlawi. Ms., IO Islamic 1450, OIOC, British Library, London. Persian text edited by Alim Ashraf Khan (Tehran: Society for the Appreciation of Cultural Works and Dignitaries, 2005). Urdu translation by Subhan Mahmud and Muhammad Fazil (New Delhi: Adabi Duniya, 1990).

Alakhbani, or *Rushdnama of Abd al-Quddus Gangohi*, Hindi translation by Saiyid Athar Abbas Rizvi and Shailesh Zaidi (Aligarh: Bharat Prakashan, 1971).

Alam, Muzaffar. *The Mughals and the Sufis: Islam and Political Imagination in India, 1500–1750* (Ranikhet: Permanent Black, 2021).

Alam, Muzaffar. *The Languages of Political Islam in India, c. 1200–1800* (New Delhi: Permanent Black, 2004).

Ali, M. Athar. *Mughal India: Studies in Polity, Ideas, Society, and Culture* (New Delhi: Oxford University Press, 2006).

Aquil, Raziuddin. *Sufism, Culture, and Politics: Afghans and Islam in Medieval North India* (New Delhi: Oxford University Press, 2007).

Aquil, Raziuddin. *The Muslim Question: Understanding Islam and Indian History* (New Delhi: Penguin Books, 2017).

Aquil, Raziuddin. *Lovers of God: Sufism and the Politics of Islam in Medieval India* (New Delhi: Manohar, 2017).

Aquil, Raziuddin (ed.). *Sufism and Society in Medieval India, Debates in Indian History and Society Series* (New Delhi: Oxford University Press, 2010).

Asher, Catherine B. and Cynthia Talbot. *India before Europe* (Cambridge: Cambridge University Press, 2006).

Auer, Blain H. *Symbols of Authority in Medieval Islam: History, Religion and Muslim Legitimacy in the Delhi Sultanate* (London and New York: I. B. Tauris, 2012).

Auer, Blain H. *In the Mirror of Persian Kings: The Origins of Perso-Islamic Courts and Empires in India* (Cambridge: Cambridge University Press, 2021).

Bazaz, Abir. *Nund Rishi: Poetry and Politics in Medieval*

Kashmir (Cambridge: Cambridge University Press, 2023).

Barani, Ziyauddin. *Fatawa-i-Jahandari, edited by Afsar Salim Khan* (Lahore: Research Society of Pakistan, 1972).

Barani, Ziyauddin. *Tarikh-i-Firuz Shahi*. English translation by Ishtiaq Ahmad Zilli (New Delhi: Primus Books, 2015).

Behl, Aditya. 'Emotion and Meaning in Mrigavat?: Strategies of Spiritual Signification in Hindavi Sufi Romances', in *After Timur Left: Culture and Circulation in Fifteenth-Century North India*, edited by rancesca Orsini and Samira Sheikh (New Delhi: Oxford University Press, 2014).

Chigateri, Shraddha. '"Glory to the Cow": Cultural Difference and Social Justice in the Food Hierarchy in India', *Journal of South Asian Studies* vol. 31, no. 1, pp. 10–35 (2008).

Chittick, William C. *Sufism: A Short Introduction* (Oxford: Oneworld Publications, 2008).

Clark, Matthew. 'Religious Sects, Syncretism, and Claims of Antiquity: The Dashanami-Sannyasis and South Asian Sufis', in *Literary and Religious Practices in Medieval and Early Modern India*, edited by Raziuddin Aquil and David L. Curley (New Delhi and London: Manohar and Routledge, 2016).

Currie, P. M. *The Shrine and Cult of Muin al-Din Chishti of Ajmer* (New Delhi: Oxford University Press, 1989).

De, Rohit. 'Cows and Constitutionalism', *Modern Asian Studies* vol. 53, no. 1, pp. 240–277 (2019).

Digby, Simon. 'Early Pilgrimages to the Graves of Muinuddin Sijzi and Other Indian Chishti Shaikhs', in Islamic Society and Culture – Essays in Honour of Aziz Ahmad, edited by M. Israel and N. K. Wagle (New Delhi: Manohar, 1983).

Digby, Simon. 'Qalandars and Related Groups: Elements of Social Deviance in the Religious Life of the Delhi Sultanate of the Thirteenth and Fourteenth Centuries', in *Islam in Asia* vol. 1, edited by Yohanan Friedman, pp. 67–8 (Jerusalem: Magnes, 1984).

Digby, Simon. 'The Sufi Shaykh as a Source of Authority in Medieval India', *Purushartha*, vol. 9, pp. 55–77 (1986).

Eaton, Richard M. *Sufis of Bijapur, 1300–1700: Social Roles of Sufis in Medieval India* (Princeton: Princeton University Press, 1978).

Eaton, Richard M. *The Rise of Islam and the Bengal Frontier* (New Delhi: Oxford University Press, 1994).

Eaton, Richard M. *Essays on Islam and Indian History* (New Delhi: Oxford University Press, 2002).

Eaton, Richard M. and Philip B. Wagoner. *Power, Memory, Architecture: Contested Sites on India's Deccan*

Plateau (New York: Oxford University Press, 2017).

Ernst, Carl W. *Eternal Garden: Mysticism, History and Politics at a South Asian Sufi Centre* (Albany: State University of New York Press, 1992).

Ernst, Carl W. and Bruce B. Lawrence. *Sufi Martyrs of Love: The Chishti Order in South Asia and Beyond* (New York: Palgrave Macmillan, 2002).

Farooqui, Amar. 'Gandhi's Spiritual Politics: Austerity, Fasting and Secularism', *Studies in History* vol. 36, no. 2, pp. 178–205 (2020).

Faruqi, Ziya-ul-Hasan. *Fawa'id al-Fu'ad: Spiritual and Literary Discourses of Shaikh Nizamuddin Awliya / Originally Compiled by Amir Hasan 'Ala' Sijzi Dehlawi*, English translation with introduction and historical annotation (New Delhi: D. K. Printworld, 1996).

Fawa'id-ul-Fu'ad, Conversations of Shaikh Nizamuddin Auliya. Compiled by Amir Hasan Sijzi. Persian text with an Urdu translation by Khwaja Hasan Sani Nizami (New Delhi: Urdu Academy, 1990).

Flatt, Emma J. *The Court of the Deccan Sultanates: Living Well in the Persian Cosmopolis* (Cambridge: Cambridge University Press, 2020).

Foltz, Richard C. *Animals in Islamic Tradition and Muslim Cultures* (Oxford: Oneworld, 2006).

Friedmann, Yohannan. *Shaykh Ahmed Sirhindi: An Outline of His Thought and a Study of His Image in the Eyes of*

Posterity (Ontario: McGill–Queen's University Press, 1972).

Gutiérrez, Andrea. 2024. 'Meat on and off the Royal Menu: The Medieval Delight of the Mind & the Erasure of Meat from Indian Recipe Collections', *Global Food History*, vol. 10, no. 2, pp. 140–58 (1972).

Habib, Mohammad. 'Chishti Mystics Records of the Sultanate Period', *Medieval India Quarterly* vol.1, pp. 1–42 (1950).

Hada, Madhav. *Kabir: Kaaljayi Kavi aur Unka Kavya* (New Delhi: Rajpal and Sons, 2022).

Hauser, Julia. *A Taste for Purity: An Entangled History of Vegetarianism* (New York: Columbia University Press, 2024).

Hess, Linda, and Sukhdev Singh. *The Bijak of Kabir* (New Delhi: Motilal Banarsidass, 2000).

Hujwiri, Shaikh Abul Hasan Ali bin. *Kashf-ul-Mahjub*, edited by Mahmud Abedi (Tehran: Soroush Press, 2013).

Hines, Naseem A. *Maulana Daud's Candayan: A Critical Study* (New Delhi: Manohar, 2009)

Jackson, Peter. *The Delhi Sultanate: A Political and Military History* (Cambridge: Cambridge University Press, 1999).

Green, Nile. *Indian Sufism since the Seventeenth Century: Saints, Books and Empires in the Muslim Deccan* (London: Routledge, 2006).

Green, Nile. *Making Space: Sufis and Settlers in Early Modern India* (New Delhi: Oxford University Press, 2012).

Habib, Irfan. *The Agrarian System of Mughal India, 1556–1707* (Bombay: Asia Publishing House, 1963); third edition in paperback (New Delhi: Oxford University Press, 2014).

Habib, Mohammad. *Politics and Society during the Early Medieval Period: Collected Works of Mohammad Habib*, vols. 1–2, edited by K. A. Nizami (New Delhi: People's Publishing House, 1974 and 1981).

Hasan, S. Nurul. *Religion, State, and Society in Medieval India*, edited and introduced by Satish Chandra (New Delhi: Oxford University Press, 2005).

Hawley, John S. *A Storm of Songs: India and the Idea of the Bhakti Movement* (Cambridge, MA: Harvard University Press, 2015).

Hoffman, Valerie. 'Eating and Fasting for God in Sufi Tradition', *Journal of the American Academy of Religion* vol. 63, pp. 465–84 (1995).

Jackson, Peter. *The Delhi Sultanate: A Political and Military History* (Cambridge: Cambridge University Press, 1999).

Jaisi, Malik Muhammad. *Padmavat*, edited with commentary by Vasudev Sharan Agarwal (Allahabad: Lokbharti Prakashan, 2010).

Juzjani, Minhaj-us Siraj. *Tabaqat-i-Nasiri* vol. 1, edited by Abdul Hayy Habibi (Kabul: Historical Society of Afghanistan, 1963–64).

Karamustafa, Ahmet T. *Sufism: The Formative Period, The New Edinburgh Islamic Surveys* (Edinburgh: Edinburgh University Press, 2007).

Kazmi, Nuzhat. *Mughal Art of Portraiture, Awraq-e Musavvir, The Intellectual Context and Content* (New Delhi: Three Essays Collective, 2021).

Keune, Jon. *Shared Devotion, Shared Food: Equality and the Bhakti-Caste Question in Western India* (New York: Oxford University Press, 2021).

Khan, Iqtidar Alam, ed. *Akbar and His Age* (New Delhi: ICHR and Northern Book Centre, 1999).

Khan, Muqtedar, and Mohammed Ayub Khan. 'Poverty in Islamic Philosophy', in *The Routledge Handbook of Philosophy and Poverty* edited by Gottfried Schweiger and Clemens Sedmak (New York: Routledge, 2023).

Khan, Maulana Wahiduddin. *Tazkirul Qur'an (A Commentary of the Qur'an in Urdu)* (New Delhi: Goodword Books, 2011).

Khair-ul-Majalis, Conversations of Shaikh Nasiruddin Chiragh-i-Dehli. Compiled by Hamid Qalandar, edited by K. A. Nizami (Aligarh: Muslim University, 1959).

Kirmani, Amir Khwurd. *Siyar-ul-Auliya* (Islamabad: Markaz Tahqiqat-i-Farsi Iran wa Pakistan, 1978).

Khusrau, Amir. *Khaza'in-ul-Futuh of Amir Khusrau*, edited by M. Wahid Mirza (Calcutta: Asiatic Society, 1953).

Kumar, Sunil. *The Emergence of the Delhi Sultanate* (New Delhi: Permanent Black, 2007).

Kugle, Scott. 'Sufi Attitude toward Homosexuality: Chishti Perspectives from South Asia', in *Literary and Religious Practices in Medieval and Early Modern India*, edited by Raziuddin Aquil and David L. Curley (New Delhi and London: Manohar and Routledge, 2016).

Kugle, Scott. 'The Chishtiyya', in *Routledge Handbook on Sufism*, edited by Lloyd Ridgeon (London: Routledge, 2020).

Lal, K. S. *The Legacy of Muslim Rule in India* (New Delhi: Aditya Prakashan, 1992).

Launay, Robert. 'Tasting the World: Food in Early European Travel Narratives', *Food and Foodways*, vol. 11, no. 1, pp. 27–47 (2003).

Lawrence, Bruce B. *Notes from a Distant Flute: The Extant Literature of Pre-Mughal Indian Sufism* (Tehran: Imperial Iranian Academy of Philosophy, 1978).

Lawrence, Bruce B. 'The Early Chishti Approach to Sama', in *Islamic Society and Culture – Essays in Honour of Professor Aziz Ahmad*, edited by M. Israel and N. K. Wagle (New Delhi: Manohar, 1983).

Lawrence, Bruce B. *Nizam Ad-Din Awliya: Morals for*

the Heart, English translation of Fawa'd-ul-Fu'ad (New York: Paulist Press, 1991).

Lorenzen, David. *Nirgun Santon Ke Swapana* (New Delhi: Rajkamal, 2010).

Maneri. Sharfuddin Yahya. *Maktubat-i-Sadi* (Patna: Khuda Bakhsh Library, 1994).

Mirza, M. Wahid. *Amir Khusrau* (Delhi: National Amir Khusrau Society, 1986).

Nizami, K. A. *The Life and Times of Nizamuddin Auliya* (New Delhi: Idarah-i Adabiyat-i Delli, 1991a).

Nizami, K. A. *The Life and Times of Shaikh Nasiruddin Chiragh* (New Delhi: Idarah-i Adabiyat-i Delli, 1991b).

Nizami, K. A. *The Life and Times of Shaikh Fariduddin Ganj-i-Shakar* (Aligarh: Aligarh Muslim University, 1955).

Nizami, Khwaja Hasan Sani. *Fawa'id-ul-Fu'ad*, Hindi translation (New Delhi: Self-published by the translator, 2004).

Norman, Corrie E. 'Food and Religion', in *The Oxford Handbook of Food History* edited by Jeffrey M. Pilcher (Oxford: Oxford University Press, pp. 409–27, 2012).

Novetzke, Christian Lee. *Religion and Public Memory: A Cultural History of Saint Namdev in India* (New York: Columbia University Press, 2008).

Pilcher, Jefferey, M. *Food in World History*, revised edition (New York: Routledge, 2023).

Qiwam, Muhammad Jamal. *Qiwam-ul-'Aqa'id*. Urdu translation by Nisar Ahmad Faruqui (Rampur, U.P.: Nashr-o-Isha'at, 1994).

Qureshi, I. H. *Ulema in Politics* (Delhi: Renaissance Publishing House, 1985).

Rajgiri, Mir Sayyid Manjhan Shattari. *Madhumalati: An Indian Sufi Romance*, translated by Aditya Behl and Simon Weightman (New Delhi: Oxford University Press, 2001).

Reynolds, Gabriel Said. 'The Sufi Approach to Food: A Case Study of Adab'. *Muslim World* vol. 90, no. 1. pp. 198–217 (2000).

Rizvi, Sayid Athar Abbas. *A History of Sufism in India, Vol. I, Early Sufism and its History in India to AD 1600* (New Delhi: Munshiram Manoharlal, 1978).

Roy, Parama. 'Meat-Eating, Masculinity, and Renunciation in India: A Gandhian Grammar of Diet', *Gender & History* vol 14. no. 2, pp. 62–91 (2002).

Salam, Ziya Us. *Lynch Files: The Forgotten Saga of Victims of Hate Crime* (New Delhi: Sage, 2019).

Schimmel, Annemarie. *The Mystical Dimensions of Islam* (Chapel Hill: University of North Carolina Press, 1975).

Sengupta, Jayanta. 'The History and Historiography of Indian Food: The State of the Field', in *Food Cultures of India*, edited by Sarit K. Chaudhuri, Debarshi

Prasad Nath and Dhurjjati Sarma (New Delhi: Manohar, 2024).

Sengupta, Jayanta. 'Bengali Mughlai Platter on the Table: Muslim and Indo-Persian Food Culture in Bengal', *Global Food History* vol. 9, no. 2, pp. 130–48 (2023).

Sharma, Sunil. *Amir Khusraw: Poet of Sultans and Sufis* (Oxford: Oneworld Publications, 2005).

Sreenivasan, Ramya. *The Many Lives of a Rajput Queen: Heroic Pasts in India, c. 1500–1900* (Seattle: University of Washington Press, 2007).

Steingass, F. *A Comprehensive Persian-English Dictionary*, reprint (New Delhi: Munshiram Manoharlal, 1996).

Syros, Vasileios. 'State Failure and Successful Leadership in Medieval India'. *Studies in History* vol. 37, no. 1, pp. 1–19 (2021).

Trivedi, Madhu. *Revisiting Hindavi Sufi Romances: Late Fourteenth to Early Sixteenth Centuries* (New Delhi: Primus Books, 2024).

Vanita, Ruth. *The Dharma of Justice in the Sanskrit Epic: Debates on Gender, Varna, and Species* (Oxford: Oxford University Press, 2022).

Vaudeville, Charlotte. *A Weaver Named Kabir – Selected Verses with a Detailed Biographical and Historical Introduction* (New Delhi: Oxford University Press, 1993).

Viitamäki, Mikko. 'Retelling Medieval History for Twentieth-century Readers: Encounter of a Hindu Prince and a Sufi Master in Khwaja Hasan Nizami's Nizami Bansuri', in *Literary and Religious Practices in Medieval and Early Modern India*, edited by Raziuddin Aquil and David L. Curley (New Delhi and London: Manohar and Routledge, 2016).

Zelliot, Eleanor, 'A Medieval Encounter Between Hindu and Muslim: Eknath's Drama Poem Hindu-Turk Samvad', in *India's Islamic Traditions*, 711–1750, edited by Richard M. Eaton (New Delhi: Oxford University Press, 2003).

Zutshi, Chitralekha. *Kashmir's Contested Pasts: Narratives, Sacred Geographies and the Historical Imagination* (New Delhi: Oxford University Press, 2014).